BASIC FUNDAMENTALS TO DOMINATE FOREX TRADING

by

JORDON SKYES

♥ Copyright 2016 by Jordon Sykes - All rights reserved.

This document is geared towards providing exact and reliable information in regards to the topic and issue covered. The publication is sold on the idea that the publisher is not required to render an accounting, officially permitted, or otherwise, qualified services. If advice is necessary, legal or professional, a practiced individual in the profession should be ordered.

- From a Declaration of Principles which was accepted and approved equally by a Committee of the American Bar Association and a Committee of Publishers and Associations.

In no way is it legal to reproduce, duplicate, or transmit any part of this document by either electronic means or in printed format. Recording of this publication is strictly prohibited and any storage of this document is not allowed unless with written permission from the publisher. All rights reserved.

The information provided herein is stated to be truthful and consistent, in that any liability, in terms of inattention or otherwise, by any usage or abuse of any policies, processes, or directions contained within is the solitary and utter responsibility of the recipient reader. Under no circumstances will any legal responsibility or blame be held against the publisher for any reparation, damages, or monetary loss due to the information herein, either directly or indirectly.

Respective authors own all copyrights not held by the publisher.

The information herein is offered for informational purposes solely and is universal as so. The presentation of the information is without a contract or any type of guarantee assurance.

The trademarks that are used are without any consent, and the publication of the trademark is without permission or backing by the trademark owner. All trademarks and brands within this book are for clarifying purposes only and are the owned by the owners themselves, not affiliated with this document.

Jordon Skyes

TABLE OF CONTENTS

INTRODUCTION

WHAT IS FOREX TRADING?

FOREIGN EXCHANGE RISKS AND BENEFITS

FOREX HISTORY AND MARKET PARTICPANTS

FUNDAMENTAL ANALYSIS AND FUNDAMENTAL TRADING STRATEGIES

COMMODITY PRICES AND CURRENCY MOVEMENTS

TECHNICAL ANALYSIS AND TECHNICAL INDICATORS

COMMON TECHNICAL INDICATORS

MOMENTUM

FOREX CONSOLIDATION

SUMMARY

Jordon Skyes

INTRODUCTION

The foreign exchange market (forex or FX for short) is one of the most exciting, fast-paced markets around. Until recently, forex trading in the currency market had been the domain of large financial institutions, corporations, central banks, hedge funds and extremely wealthy individuals. The emergence of the internet has changed all of this, and now it is possible for average investors to buy and sell currencies easily with the click of a mouse through online brokerage accounts.

Daily currency fluctuations are usually very small. Most currency pairs move less than one cent per day, representing a less than 1% change in the value of the currency. This makes foreign exchange one of the least volatile financial markets around. Therefore, many currency speculators rely on the availability of enormous leverage to increase the value of potential movements. In the retail forex market, leverage can be as much as 250:1. Higher leverage can be extremely risky, but because of round-the-clock trading and deep liquidity, foreign exchange brokers have been able to make high leverage an industry standard in order to make the movements meaningful for currency traders.

Extreme liquidity and the availability of high leverage have helped to spur the market's rapid growth and made it the ideal place for many traders. Positions can be opened and closed within minutes or can be held for months. Currency prices are based on objective considerations of supply and demand and cannot be manipulated easily because the size of the market does not allow even the largest players, such as central banks, to move prices at will.

The forex market provides plenty of opportunity for investors. However, in order to be successful, a currency trader has to understand the basics behind currency movements.

The goal of this forex ebook is to provide a foundation for investors or traders who are new to the foreign currency markets. We'll cover the basics of exchange rates, the market's history and the key concepts you need to understand in order to be able to participate in this market. We'll also venture into how to start trading foreign currencies and the different types of strategies that can be employed.

Jordon Skyes

CHAPTER ONE

WHAT IS FOREX TRADING?

The foreign exchange market is the "place" where currencies are traded. Currencies are important to most people around the world, whether they realize it or not, because currencies need to be exchanged in order to conduct foreign trade and business. If you are living in the U.S. and want to buy cheese from France, either you or the company that you buy the cheese from has to pay the French for the cheese in euros (EUR). This means that the U.S. importer would have to exchange the equivalent value of U.S. dollars (USD) into euros. The same goes for traveling. A French tourist in Egypt can't pay in euros to see the pyramids because it's not the locally accepted currency. As such, the tourist has to exchange the euros for the local currency, in this case, the Egyptian pound, at the current exchange rate.

The need to exchange currencies is the primary reason why the forex market is the largest, most liquid financial market in the world. It dwarfs other markets in size, even the stock market, with an average traded value of around U.S. $2,000 billion per day. (The total volume changes all the time, but as of August 2012, the Bank for International Settlements (BIS) reported that the forex market traded in excess of U.S. $4.9 trillion per day.)

One unique aspect of this international market is that there is no central marketplace for foreign exchange. Rather, currency trading is conducted electronically over-the-counter (OTC), which means that all transactions occur via computer networks between traders around the world, rather than on one centralized exchange. The market is open 24 hours a day, five and a half days a week, and currencies are traded worldwide in the major financial centers of London, New York, Tokyo, Zurich, Frankfurt, Hong Kong, Singapore, Paris, and Sydney - across almost every time zone. This means that when the trading day in the U.S. ends, the forex market begins anew in Tokyo and Hong Kong. As such, the forex market can be extremely active any time of the day, with price quotes changing constantly.

Spot Market and the Forwards and Futures Markets

There are actually three ways that institutions, corporations, and individuals trade forex: the spot market, the forwards market and the futures market. The forex trading in the spot market always has been the largest market because it is the "underlying" real asset that the forwards and futures markets are based on. In the past, the futures market was the most popular venue for traders because it was available to individual investors for a longer period of time. However, with the advent of electronic trading, the spot market has witnessed a huge surge in activity and now surpasses the futures market as the preferred trading market for individual investors and speculators. When people refer to the forex market, they usually are referring to the spot market. The forwards and futures markets tend to be more popular with companies that need to hedge their foreign exchange risks out to a specific date in the future.

What is the spot market?

More specifically, the spot market is where currencies are bought and sold according to the current price. That price, determined by supply and demand, is a reflection of many things, including current interest rates, economic performance, sentiment towards ongoing political situations (both locally and internationally), as well as the perception of the future performance of one currency against another. When a deal is finalized, this is known as a "spot deal". It is a bilateral transaction by which one party delivers an agreed-upon currency amount to the counterparty and receives a specified amount of another currency at the agreed-upon exchange rate value. After a position is closed, the settlement is in cash. Although the spot market is commonly known as one that deals with transactions in the present (rather than the future), these trades actually take two days for settlement.

What are the forwards and futures markets?

Unlike the spot market, the forwards and futures markets do not trade actual currencies. Instead, they deal in contracts that represent claims to a certain currency type, a specific price per unit and a future date for settlement.

In the forwards market, contracts are bought and sold OTC between two parties, who determine the terms of the agreement between themselves.

In the futures market, futures contracts are bought and sold based upon a standard size and settlement date on public commodities markets, such as the Chicago Mercantile Exchange. In the U.S., the National Futures Association regulates the futures market. Futures contracts have specific details, including the number of units being traded, delivery and settlement dates, and minimum price increments that cannot be customized. The exchange acts as a counterpart to the trader, providing clearance and settlement.

Both types of contracts are binding and are typically settled for cash for the exchange in question upon expiry, although contracts can also be bought and sold before they expire. The forwards and futures markets can offer protection against risk when trading currencies. Usually, big international corporations use these markets in order to hedge against future exchange rate fluctuations, but speculators take part in these markets as well.

FOREIGN EXCHANGE RISKS AND BENEFITS

The Good and the Bad

We already have mentioned that factors such as the size, volatility and global structure of the foreign exchange market have all contributed to its rapid success. Given the highly liquid nature of this market, investors are able to place extremely large trades without affecting any given exchange rate. These large positions are made available to forex traders because of the low margin requirements used by the majority of the industry's brokers. For example, it is possible for a trader to control a position of US$100,000 by putting down as little as US$1,000 up front and borrowing the remainder from his or her forex broker. This amount of leverage acts as a double-edged sword because investors can realize large gains when rates make a small favorable change, but they also run the risk of a massive loss when the rates move against them. Despite the foreign exchange risks, the amount of leverage available in the forex market is what makes it attractive for many speculators.

The currency market is also the only market that is truly open 24 hours a day with decent liquidity throughout the day. For traders who may have a day job or just a busy schedule, it is an optimal market to trade in. As you can see from the chart below, the major trading hubs are spread throughout many different time zones, eliminating the need to wait for an opening or closing bell. As the U.S. trading closes, other markets in the East are opening, making it possible to trade at any time during the day.

Time Zone	Time (ET)
Tokyo Open	7:00 pm
Tokyo Close	4:00 am
London Open	3:00 am
London Close	12:00 pm
New York Open	8:00 am
New York Close	5:00 pm

While the forex market may offer more excitement to the investor, the risks are also higher in comparison to trading equities. The ultra-high leverage of the forex market means that huge gains can quickly turn to damaging losses and can wipe out the majority of your account in a matter of minutes. This is important for all new traders to understand, because in the forex market - due to a large amount of money involved and the number of players - traders will react quickly to information released into the market, leading to sharp moves in the price of the currency pair.

Though currencies don't tend to move as sharply as equities on a percentage basis (where a company's stock can lose a large portion of its value in a matter of minutes after a bad announcement), it is the leverage in the spot market that creates the volatility. For example, if you are using 100:1 leverage on $1,000 invested, you control $100,000 in capital. If you put $100,000 into a currency and the currency's price moves 1% against you, the value of the capital will have decreased to $99,000 - a loss of $1,000, or all of your invested capital, representing a 100% loss. In the equities market, most traders do not use leverage, therefore a 1% loss in the stock's value on a $1,000 investment, would only mean a loss of $10. Therefore, it is important to take into account the risks involved in the forex market before diving in.

Differences Between Forex and Equities

A major difference between the forex and equities markets is the number of traded instruments: the forex market has very few compared to the thousands found in the equities market. The majority of forex traders focus their efforts on seven different currency pairs: the four majors, which include (EUR/USD, USD/JPY, GBP/USD, USD/CHF); and the three commodity pairs (USD/CAD, AUD/USD, NZD/USD). All other pairs are just different combinations of the same currencies, otherwise known as cross currencies. This makes currency trading easier to follow because rather than having to cherry-pick between

10,000 stocks to find the best value, all that FX traders need to do is "keep up" on the economic and political news of eight countries.

The equity markets often can hit a lull, resulting in shrinking volumes and activity. As a result, it may be hard to open and close positions when desired. Furthermore, in a declining market, it is only with the extreme ingenuity that an equities investor can make a profit. It is difficult to short-sell in the U.S. equities market because of strict rules and regulations regarding the process. On the other hand, forex offers the opportunity to profit in both rising and declining markets because with each trade, you are buying and selling simultaneously, and short-selling is, therefore, inherent in every transaction. In addition, since the forex market is so liquid, traders are not required to wait for an uptick before they are allowed to enter into a short position - as they are in the equities market.

Due to the extreme liquidity of the forex market, margins are low and leverage is high. It just is not possible to find such low margin rates in the equities markets; most margin traders in the equities markets need at least 50% of the value of the investment available as margin, whereas forex traders need as little as 1%. Furthermore, commissions in the equities market are much higher than in the forex market. Traditional brokers ask for commission fees on top of the spread, plus the fees that have to be paid to the exchange. Spot forex brokers take only the spread as their fee for the transaction. (For a more in-depth introduction to currency trading,

Jordon Skyes

FOREX HISTORY AND MARKET PARTICIPANTS

Given the global nature of the forex exchange market, it is important to first examine and learn some of the important historical events relating to currencies and currency exchange before entering any trades. In this section, we'll review the international monetary system and how it has evolved to its current state. We will then take a look at the major players that occupy the forex market - something that is important for all potential forex traders to understand.

The History of the Forex

Gold Standard System

The creation of the gold standard monetary system in 1875 marks one of the most important events in the history of the forex market. Before the gold standard was implemented, countries would commonly use gold and silver as means of international payment. The main issue with using gold and silver for payment is that their value is affected by external supply and demand. For example, the discovery of a new gold mine would drive gold prices down.

The underlying idea behind the gold standard was that governments guaranteed the conversion of currency into a specific amount of gold, and vice versa. In other words, a currency would be backed by gold. Obviously, governments needed a fairly substantial gold reserve in order to meet the demand for currency exchanges. During the late nineteenth century, all of the major economic countries had defined an amount of currency to an ounce of gold. Over time, the difference in price of an ounce of gold between two currencies became the exchange rate for those two currencies. This represented the first standardized means of currency exchange in history.

The gold standard eventually broke down during the beginning of World War I. Due to the political tension with Germany, the major European powers felt a need to complete large military projects. The financial burden of these projects was so substantial that there was not enough gold at the time to exchange for all the excess currency that the governments were printing off.

Although the gold standard would make a small comeback during the inter-war years, most countries had dropped it again by the onset of World War II. However, gold never ceased being the ultimate form of monetary value. (For more on this, read The Gold Standard Revisited, What Is Wrong With Gold? and Using Technical Analysis In The Gold Markets.)

Bretton Woods System

Before the end of World War II, the Allied nations believed that there would be a need to set up a monetary system in order to fill the void that was left behind when the gold standard system was abandoned. In July 1944, more than 700 representatives from the Allies convened at Bretton Woods, New Hampshire, to deliberate over what would be called the Bretton Woods system of international monetary management.

To simplify, Bretton Woods led to the formation of the following:

A method of fixed exchange rates;

The U.S. dollar replacing the gold standard to become a primary reserve currency; and

The creation of three international agencies to oversee economic activity: the International Monetary Fund (IMF), International Bank for Reconstruction and Development, and the General Agreement on Tariffs and Trade (GATT).

One of the main features of Bretton Woods is that the U.S. dollar replaced gold as the main standard of convertibility for the world's currencies; and furthermore, the U.S. dollar became the only currency that would be backed by gold. (This turned out to be the primary reason that Bretton Woods eventually failed.)

Over the next 25 or so years, the U.S. had to run a series of balance of payment deficits in order to be the world's reserve currency. By the early 1970s, U.S. gold reserves were so depleted that the U.S. treasury did not have enough gold to cover all the U.S. dollars that foreign central banks had in reserve.

Finally, on August 15, 1971, U.S. President Richard Nixon closed the gold window, and the U.S. announced to the world that it would no longer exchange gold for the U.S. dollars that were held in foreign reserves. This event marked the end of Bretton Woods.

Even though Bretton Woods didn't last, it left an important legacy that still has a significant effect on today's international economic climate. This legacy exists in the form of the three international agencies created in the 1940s: the IMF, the International Bank for Reconstruction and Development (now part of the World Bank) and GATT, the precursor to the World Trade Organization. (To learn more about Bretton Wood, read What Is The International Monetary Fund? and Floating And Fixed Exchange Rates.)

Current Exchange Rates

After the Bretton Woods system broke down, the world finally accepted the use of floating foreign exchange rates during the Jamaica agreement of 1976. This meant that the use of the gold standard would be permanently abolished. However, this is not to say that governments adopted a pure free-floating exchange rate system. Most governments employ one of the following three exchange rate systems that are still used today:

- Dollarization;
- Pegged rate; and
- Managed floating rate.

Dollarization

This event occurs when a country decides not to issue its own currency and adopts a foreign currency as its national currency. Although dollarization usually enables a country to be seen as a more stable place for investment, the drawback is that the country's central bank can no longer print money or make any sort of monetary policy.

FUNDAMENTAL ANALYSIS AND FUNDAMENTAL TRADING STRATEGIES

In the equities market, the fundamental analysis looks to measure a company's true value and to base investments on this type of calculation. To some extent, the same is done in the retail forex market, where forex fundamental traders evaluate currencies, and their countries, like companies and use economic announcements to gain an idea of the currency's true value.

All of the news reports, economic data and political events that come out about a country are similar to news that comes out of a stock in that it is used by investors to gain an idea of value. This value changes over time due to many factors, including economic growth and financial strength. Fundamental traders look at all of this information to evaluate a country's currency.

Given that there are practically unlimited forex fundamentals trading strategies based on fundamental data, one could write a book on this subject. To give you a better idea of a tangible trading opportunity, let's go over one of the most well-known situations, the forex carry trade. (To read some frequently asked questions about currency trading, see Common Questions About Currency Trading.)

A Breakdown of the Forex Carry Trade

The currency carries trade is a strategy in which a trader sells a currency that is offering lower interest rates and purchases a currency that offers a higher interest rate. In other words, you borrow at a low rate and then lend at a higher rate. The trader using the strategy captures the difference between the two rates. When highly leveraging the trade, even a small difference between two rates can make the trade highly profitable. Along with capturing the rate difference, investors also will often see the value of the higher currency rise as money flows into the higher-yielding currency, which bids up its value.

Real-life examples of a yen carry trade can be found starting in 1999 when Japan decreased its interest rates to almost zero. Investors would capitalize on these lower interest rates and borrow a large sum of Japanese yen. The borrowed yen is then converted into U.S. dollars, which are used to buy U.S. Treasury bonds with yields and coupons at around 4.5-5%. Since the Japanese interest rate was essentially zero, the investor would be paying next to nothing to borrow the Japanese yen and earn almost all the yield on his or her U.S. Treasury bonds. But with leverage, you can greatly increase the return.

For example, 10 times leverage would create a return of 30% on a 3% yield. If you have $1,000 in your account and have access to 10 times leverage, you will control $10,000. If you implement the currency carry trade from the example above, you will earn 3% per year. At the end of the year, your $10,000 investment would equal $10,300, or a $300 gain. Because you only invested $1,000 of your own money, your real return would be 30% ($300/$1,000). However, this strategy only works if the currency pair's value remains unchanged or appreciates. Therefore, most forex carries trades look not only to earn the interest rate differential, but also capital appreciation. While we've greatly simplified this transaction, the key thing to remember here is that a small difference in interest rates can result in huge gains when leverage is applied. Most currency brokers require a minimum margin to earn interest for carry trades.

However, this transaction is complicated by changes in the exchange rate between the two countries. If the lower-yielding currency appreciates against the higher-yielding currency, the gain earned between the two yields could be eliminated. The major reason that this can happen is that the risks of the higher-yielding currency are too much for investors, so they choose to invest in the lower-yielding, safer currency. Because carry trades are longer term in nature, they are susceptible to a variety of changes over time, such as rising rates in the lower-yielding currency, which attracts more investors and can lead to currency appreciation, diminishing the returns of the carry trade. This makes the future direction of the currency pair just as important as the interest rate differential itself. (To read more about currency pairs, see Using Currency Correlations To Your Advantage, Making Sense Of The Euro/Swiss Franc Relationship and Forces Behind Exchange Rates.)

To clarify this further, imagine that the interest rate in the U.S. was 5%, while the same interest rate in Russia was 10%, providing a carry trade opportunity for traders to short the U.S. dollar and to long the Russian ruble. Assume the trader borrows $1,000 US at 5% for a year and converts it into Russian rubles at a rate of 25 USD/RUB (25,000 rubles), investing the proceeds for a year. Assuming no currency changes, the 25,000 rubles grows to 27,500 and, if converted back to U.S. dollars, will be worth $1,100 US. But because the trader borrowed $1,000 US at 5%, he or she owes $1,050 US, making the net proceeds of the trade only $50.

However, imagine that there was another crisis in Russia, such as the one that was seen in 1998 when the Russian government defaulted on its debt and there was large currency devaluation in Russia as market participants sold off their Russian currency positions. If at the end of the year the exchange rate was 50 USD/RUB, your 27,500 rubles would now convert into only $550 US (27,500 RUB x 0.02 RUB/USD). Because the trader owes $1,050 US, he or she will have lost a significant percentage of the original investment on this carry trade because of the currency's fluctuation - even though the interest rates in Russia were higher than the U.S.

COMMODITY PRICES AND CURRENCY MOVEMENTS

Predicting the next move in the markets is the key to making money in trading, but putting this simple concept into action is much harder than it sounds. Professional forex traders have long known that trading currencies require looking beyond the world of FX. The fact is that currencies are moved by many factors - supply and demand, politics, interest rates, economic growth, and so on. More specifically, since economic growth and exports are directly related to a country\'s domestic industry, it is natural for some currencies to be heavily correlated with commodity prices. The top three currencies that have the tightest correlations with commodities are the Australian dollar, the Canadian dollar, and the New Zealand dollar. Other currencies that are also impacted by commodity prices but have a weaker correlation are the Swiss franc and the Japanese yen. Knowing which currency is correlated with what commodity can help traders understand and predict certain market movements. Here we look at currencies correlated with oil and gold and show you how you can use this information in your trading.

Top 10 Forex Trading Rules

Oil and the Canadian Dollar

Over the past few years, the price of commodities has fluctuated significantly. Oil, for example, surged from $60 a barrel in 2006 to a high of $147.27 a barrel in 2008 before plummeting back below $40 a barrel in the first quarter of 2009 and rising to above $80 in 2011. Similar volatility can be seen in the price of gold , which hit $1600 an ounce in June 2011 and then a new high of over $1,800 an ounce a few months later in August 2011. With many countries around the world in recession, the trend of commodity prices can mean the difference between a deeper downturn and a faster recovery. Knowing which currencies are affected by what commodities will help you make more educated trading decisions. (Find out how the everyday items you use can affect your investments in Commodities That Move The Markets.)

Oil is one of the world\'s basic necessities - at least for now, most people in developed countries cannot live without it. In February 2009, the price of oil was nearly 70% below its all-time high of $147.27 set on July 11, 2008. A decline in oil prices is a nightmare for oil producers, while oil consumers enjoy the benefits of greater purchasing power. This is a complete 180-degree change from the situation at the beginning of 2008 when record-high oil prices put a big smile on the faces of oil producers while forcing oil consumers to pinch pennies. There are a number of reasons to explain the fall in oil prices, including a stronger dollar (oil is priced in dollars) and weaker global demand. As a net oil exporter, Canada is severely hurt by declines in oil, while Japan - a major net oil importer - tends to benefit.

Between the years 2006-2009, for example, the correlation between the Canadian dollar and oil prices was approximately 80%. On a day-to-day basis, the correlation can break, but over the long term, it has been strong because the value of the Canadian dollar has good reason to be sensitive to the price of oil. Canada is the seventh-largest producer of crude oil in the world and continues to climb up the list, with production in oil sands increasing regularly. In 2000, Canada surpassed Saudi Arabia as the United States\' most significant oil supplier. Unbeknownst to many, the size of Canada\'s oil reserves is second only to those in Saudi Arabia. The geographical proximity between the U.S. and Canada, as well as the growing political uncertainty in the Middle East and South America, makes Canada one of the most desirable places from which the U.S. can import oil. But Canada does not service only U.S. demand. The country\'s vast oil resources are beginning to get a lot of attention from China, especially since Canada stumbled upon a new stash of oil after a reclassification of its Alberta oil sands to the "economically recoverable" category. (Read more in Peak Oil: What To Do When The Wells Run Dry.)

Figure 1 shows the clearly positive relationship between oil and the Canadian loonie. In fact, it should come as no surprise that the price of oil actually acts as a leading indicator for the price action of the CAD/USD. Since the traded instrument is the inverse, or USD/CAD, it's important to note that based on the historical relationship, when oil prices go up, USD/CAD falls and when oil prices go down USD/CAD rises.

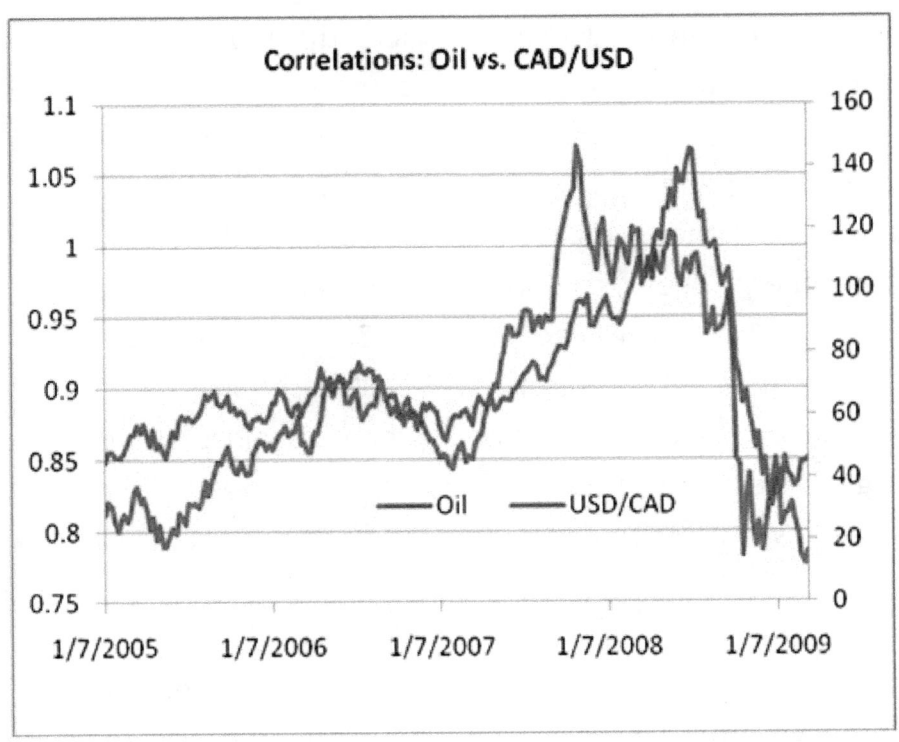

Figure 1: A look at the correlation between the price of oil and the price action in

the CAD/USD from January 2005 to March 2009

Oil and the Japanese Economy

At the other end of the spectrum is Japan, which imports nearly all of its oil (compared to the U.S., which imports approximately 50%). As of 2011, it is the world\'s third largest net oil importer behind the U.S. and China. Japan\'s lack of domestic sources of energy, and its need to import vast amounts of crude oil, natural gas, and other energy resources, make it particularly sensitive to changes in oil prices. Japan also lacks the flexibility to switch to nuclear power because it is a huge net importer of uranium for its nuclear power plants. As of 2008, the country\'s dependence on imports for primary energy stood at more than 84%. Oil provided Japan with 49% of its total energy needs, coal with 20%, nuclear power 13%, natural gas 14%, hydroelectric power 3% and renewable sources a mere 1%. Therefore, when oil prices skyrocket, the Japanese economy suffers. (Hedge against rising energy prices and diversify your portfolio; read ETFs Provide Easy Access To Energy Commodities.)

An Attractive Oil Play: CAD/JPY

Looking at this from a net oil exporter/importer perspective, the currency pair that tops the list of currencies to trade to express a view on oil prices is the Canadian dollar against the Japanese yen. Figure 2 illustrates the tight correlation between oil prices and CAD/JPY. More often than not, oil prices tend to be the leading indicator (as with USD/CAD) for CAD/JPY price action with a noticeable delay. As oil prices continued to fall during this period, CAD/JPY broke the 100 level to hit a low of 76.

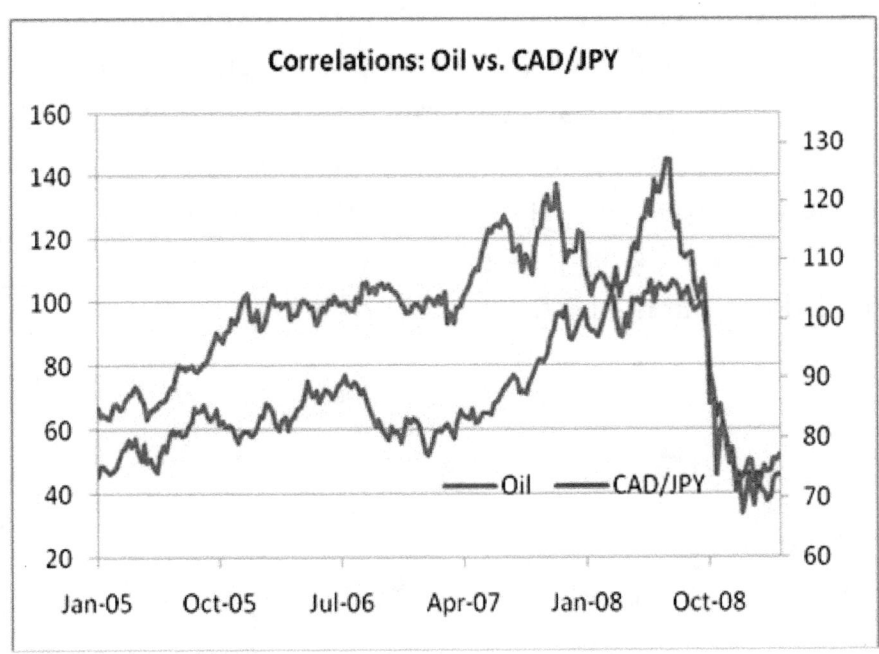

Figure 2: A look at the correlation between the price of oil and the price action in the CAD/JPY from January 2005 to March 2009

Going for Gold

Gold traders may also be surprised to hear that trading the Australian dollar is just like trading gold in many ways. As the world's third-largest producer of gold, the Australian dollar had an 84% positive correlation with the precious metal between 1999 and 2008. Generally speaking, this means that when gold prices rise, the Australian dollar appreciates as well. The proximity of New Zealand to Australia makes Australia a preferred destination for exporting New Zealand goods. Therefore, the health of New Zealand's economy is closely tied to the health of the Australian economy, which explains why the NZD/USD and the AUD/USD have had a 96% positive correlation over the same time period. The correlation of the NZD/USD with gold is slightly less than that of the Australia dollar but is still strong at 78%.

Figure 3: A look at the correlation between the price of gold and the price action in the NZD/USD from January 2005 to March 2009

A weaker, but still important, correlation is that of gold prices and the Swiss franc. The country's political neutrality and the fact that its currency used to be backed by gold have made the franc the currency of choice in times of political uncertainty. From January 2006 until January 2009, USD/CHF and gold prices had a 77% positive correlation. However, the relationship broke down somewhat in September 2005 as the U.S. dollar decoupled from gold price movements. (For further reading, see The Gold Standard Revisited and What Is Wrong With Gold?)

Trading Currencies as a Supplement to Trading Oil or Gold

For seasoned commodity traders, it may also be worthwhile to look at trading currencies as an alternative or a supplement to trading commodities. In addition to being able to capitalize on a similar outlook (e.g. higher oil), traders may also be able to earn interest if they are on 2% margin or higher with most brokers. When trading currencies, you are dealing with countries, and countries have interest rates, of course. For example, a trader who may have bought the AUD/USD in March 2009 would be able to earn up to 3% in interest income if Australian interest rates remained at 3.25% and U.S. interest rates remained at 0.25% for the entire year. The 3% comes from taking Australia's central bank rate, which is the amount earned and subtracting the nearly 0% rates paid for shorting the U.S. dollar. These are unleveraged rates, which mean that with 10 times leverage, for example, net of any exchange rate changes, the interest income would be that much higher. Leverage also makes the trade riskier, which means that if the trade turns against you, losses will be larger.

Along the same lines, if you shorted AUD/USD to express a short gold view, you would end up paying interest. If you're a commodity trader looking for a bit of a change from the usual pro gold trade (for example), commodity currencies such as the AUD/USD and NZD/USD provide good opportunities worth looking into.

Conclusion

If you want to trade commodity currencies, the best way to use commodity prices in your trading is to always keep one eye on movements in the oil or gold market and the other eye on the currency market to watch how quickly it responds. Due to the slightly delayed impact of these movements on the currency market, there is generally an opportunity to overlay a broader movement that is happening in the commodity market to that of the currency market. Bottom line: It never hurts to be more informed about commodity prices and how they drive currency movements.

TECHNICAL ANALYSIS AND TECHNICAL INDICATORS

One of the underlying tenets of technical analysis is that historical price action predicts future price action. Since the forex is a 24-hour market, there tends to be a large amount of data that can be used to gauge future price activity, thereby increasing the statistical significance of the forecast. This makes it the perfect market for traders that use technical tools, such as trends, charts, and indicators. (To learn more, see Introduction to Technical Analysis and Charting Your Way To Better Returns.)

It is important to note that, in general, the interpretation of technical analysis remains the same regardless of the asset being monitored. There are literally hundreds of books dedicated to this field of study, but in this tutorial, we will only touch on the basics of why technical analysis is such a popular tool in the forex market.

As the specific techniques of technical analysis are discussed in other tutorials, we will focus on the most forex-specific aspects of technical analysis.

Technical Analysis Discounts Everything; Especially in Forex

Minimal Rate Inconsistency

There are many large players in the forex market, such as hedge funds and large banks, that all have advanced computer systems to constantly monitor any inconsistencies between the different currency pairs. Given these programs, it is rare to see any major inconsistency last longer than a matter of seconds. Many traders turn to forex technical analysis because it presumes that all the factors that influence a price - economic, political, social and psychological - have already been factored into the current exchange rate by the market. With so many investors and so much money exchanging hands each day, the trend and flow of capital are what becomes important, rather than attempting to identify a mispriced rate.

Trend or Range

One of the greatest goals of technical traders in the FX market is to determine whether a given pair will trend in a certain direction, or if it will travel sideways and remain range-bound. The most common method to determine these characteristics is to draw trend lines that connect historical levels that have prevented a rate from heading higher or lower. These levels of support and resistance are used by technical traders to determine whether or not the given trend, or lack of trend, will continue.

Generally, the major currency pairs - such as the EUR/USD, USD/JPY, USD/CHF and GBP/USD - have shown the greatest characteristics of trend, while the currency pairs that have historically shown a higher probability of becoming range-bound have been the currency crosses (pairs not involving the U.S. dollar). The two charts below show the strong trending nature of USD/JPY in contrast to the range-bound nature of EUR/CHF. It is important for every trader to be aware of the characteristics of trend and range because they will not only affect what pairs are traded, but also what type of strategy should be used.

FIGURE 1

Figure 2

Jordon Skyes

COMMON TECHNICAL INDICATORS

Technical traders use many different indicators in combination with support and resistance to aid them in predicting the future direction of exchange rates. Again, learning how to interpret various forex technical indicators is a study unto itself and goes beyond the scope of this forex tutorial.

A few indicators that we feel we should mention, due to their popularity, are Bollinger Bands®, Fibonacci retracement, moving averages, moving average convergence divergence (MACD) and stochastics. These technical tools are rarely used by themselves to generate signals, but rather in conjunction with other indicators and chart patterns.

USING BOLLINGER BANDS TO GUAGE TRENDS

Bollinger Bands are one of the most popular technical indicators for traders in any financial market, whether investors are trading stocks, bonds or foreign exchange (FX). Many traders use Bollinger Bands® to determine overbought and oversold levels, selling when price touches the upper Bollinger Band® and buying when it hits the lower Bollinger Band®. In range-bound markets, this technique works well, as prices travel between the two bands like balls bouncing off the walls of a racquetball court. However, Bollinger Bands® don't always give accurate buy and sell signals. This is where the more specific Bollinger Band® "bands" come in. Let's take a look.

Analyzing Chart Patterns

The Problem With Bollinger Bands®

As John Bollinger was first to acknowledge, "tags of the bands are just that - tags, not signals. A tag of the upper Bollinger Band® is not in and of itself a sell signal. A tag of the lower Bollinger Band® is not in and of itself a buy signal". Price often can and does "walk the band". In those markets, traders who continuously try to "sell the top" or "buy the bottom" are faced with an excruciating series of stop-outs or worse, an ever-mounting floating loss as price moves further and further away from the original entry.

Perhaps a more useful way to trade with Bollinger Bands® is to use them to gauge trends. To understand why Bollinger Bands® may be a good tool for this task we first need to ask - what is a trend?

Trend as Deviance

One standard cliché in trading is that prices range 80% of the time. Like many clichés, this one contains a good amount of truth since markets mostly consolidate as bulls and bear battle for supremacy. Market trends are rare, which is why trading them is not nearly as easy as it seems. Looking at the price this way we can then define a trend as a deviation from the norm (range).

The Bollinger Band® formula consists of the following:

BOLU = Upper Bollinger Band®

BOLD = Lower Bollinger Band®

n = Smoothing Period

m = Number of Standard Deviations (SD)

SD = Standard Deviation over Last n Periods Typical Price (TP) = (HI + LO + CL) / 3

BOLU = MA(TP, n) + m * SD[TP, n]

BOLD = MA(TP, n) - m * SD[TP, n]

At the core, Bollinger Bands® measure deviation. This is the reason why they can be very helpful in diagnosing trend. By generating two sets of Bollinger Bands® - one set using the parameter of "1 standard deviation" and the other using the typical setting of "2 standard deviations" - we can look at the price in a whole new way.

In the chart below we see that whenever price channels between the upper Bollinger Bands® +1 SD and +2 SD away from mean, the trend is up; therefore, we can define that channel as the "buy zone". Conversely, if price channels within Bollinger Bands® −1 SD and −2 SD, it is in the "sell zone". Finally, if price meanders between +1 SD band and −1 SD band, it is essentially in a neutral state, and we can say that it's in "no man's land".

One of the other great advantages of Bollinger Bands® is that they adapt dynamically to price expanding and contracting as volatility increases and decreases. Therefore, the bands naturally widen and narrow in sync with price action, creating a very accurate trending envelope.

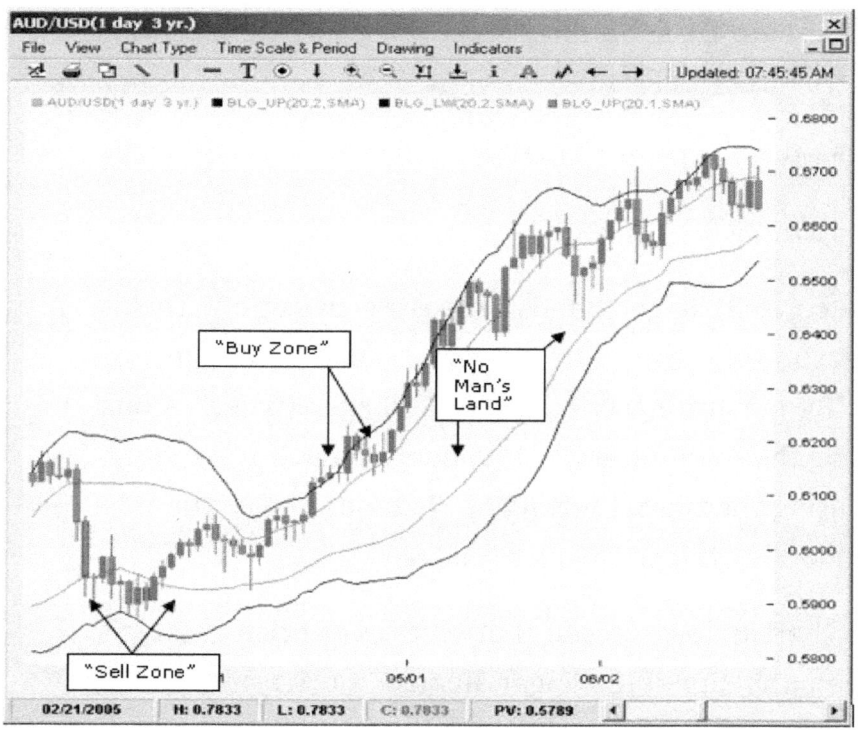

Figure 1: Bollinger Band® channels show trends

A Tool for Trend Traders and Faders

Having established the basic rules for Bollinger Band® "bands", we can now demonstrate how this technical tool can be used by both trend traders who seek to exploit momentum and fade traders who like to profit from trend exhaustion. Returning back to the AUD/USD chart just above, we can see how trend traders would position long once price entered the "buy zone". They would then be able to stay in trend as the Bollinger Band® "bands" encapsulate most of the price action of the massive up-move.

What would the logical stop-out point be? The answer is different for each individual trader, but one reasonable possibility would be to close the long trade if the candle turned red and more than 75% of its body were below the "buy zone". Using the 75% rule is obvious since at that point price clearly falls out of trend, but why insist that the candle is red? The reason for the second condition is to prevent the trend trader from being "wiggled out" of a trend by a quick probative move to the downside that snaps back to the "buy zone" at the end of the trading period. Note how in the following chart the trader is able to stay on the move for most of the uptrend, exiting only when the price starts to consolidate at the top of the new range.

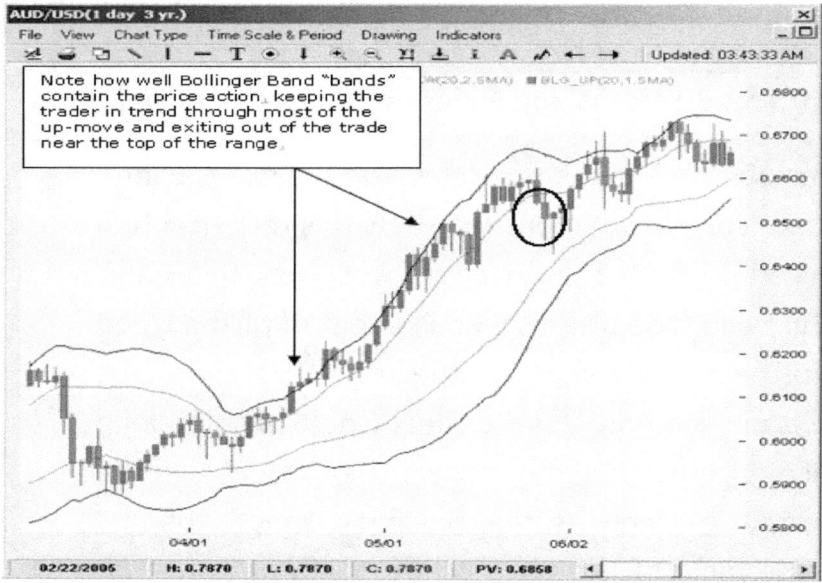

Figure 2: Bollinger Band® "bands" contain price action

Bollinger Band® "bands" can also be a valuable tool for traders who like to exploit trend exhaustion by picking the turn in price. Note, however, that counter-trend trading requires far larger margins of error as trends will often make several attempts at continuation before capitulating.

In the chart below, we see that a fade trader using Bollinger Band® "bands" will be able to quickly diagnose the first hint of trend weakness. Having seen prices fall out of the trend channel, the fader may decide to make classic use of Bollinger Bands® by shorting the next tag of the upper Bollinger Band®. But where to place the stop? Putting it just above the swing high will practically assure the trader of a stop-out as the price will often make many probative forays to the top of the range, with buyers trying to extend the trend. Here is where the volatility property of Bollinger Bands® becomes an enormous benefit to the trader. By measuring the width of the "no man's land" area, which is simply the range of +1 to –1 SD from the mean, the trader can create a quick and very effective projection zone, which will prevent him from being stopped out on market noise and yet protect his capital if trend truly regains its momentum.

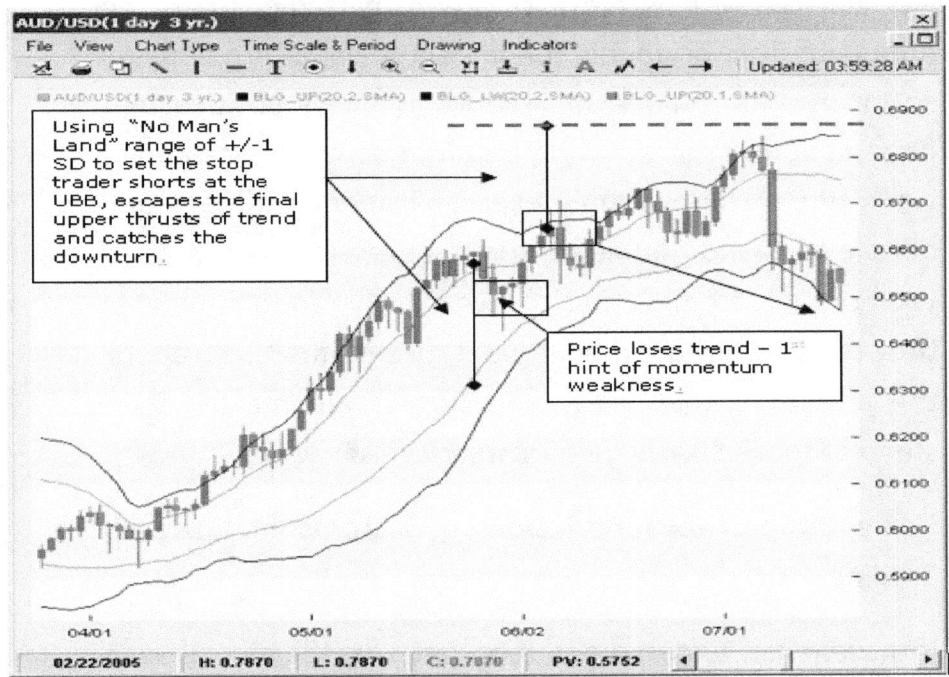

Figure 3: Fade trading using Bollinger Band® "bands"

The Bottom Line

As one the most popular technical analysis indicators, Bollinger Bands® have become crucial for many technically oriented traders. By extending their functionality through the use of Bollinger Band® "bands", traders can achieve a greater level of analytical sophistication using this simple and elegant tool for both trending and fading strategies.

TRADING DOUBLE TOPS AND DOUBLE BOTTOMS

No chart pattern is more common in trading than the double bottom or double top. In fact, this pattern appears so often that it alone may serve as proof positive that price action is not as wildly random as many academics claim. Price charts simply express trader sentiment and double tops and double bottoms represent a retesting of temporary extremes. If prices were truly random, why do they pause so frequently at just those points? To traders, the answer is that many participants are making their stand at those clearly demarcated levels.

Using Double Tops And Double Bottoms In Currency Trading

If these levels undergo and repel attacks, they instill even more confidence in the traders who've defended the barrier and, as such, are likely to generate strong profitable countermoves. Here we look at the difficult task of spotting the important double bottom and double tops, and we demonstrate how Bollinger Bands® can help you set appropriate stops when you're trading these patterns.

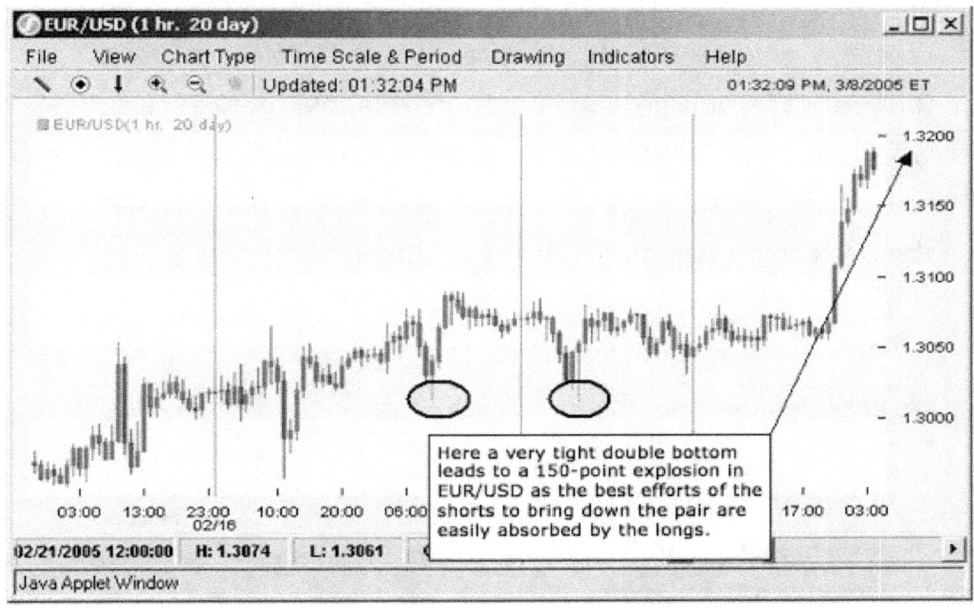

React or Anticipate?

One great criticism of technical pattern trading is that setups always look obvious in hindsight but that executing in real time is actually very difficult. Double tops and double bottoms are no exceptions. Although these patterns appear almost daily, successfully identifying and trading the patterns is no easy task.

A Trader's Guide To Using Fractals

There are two approaches to this problem and both have their merits and drawbacks. In short, traders can either anticipate these formations or wait for confirmation and react to them. Which approach you chose is more a function of your personality than relative merit. Those who have a fader mentality - who love to fight the tape, sell into strength and buy weakness - will try to anticipate the pattern by stepping in front of the price move.

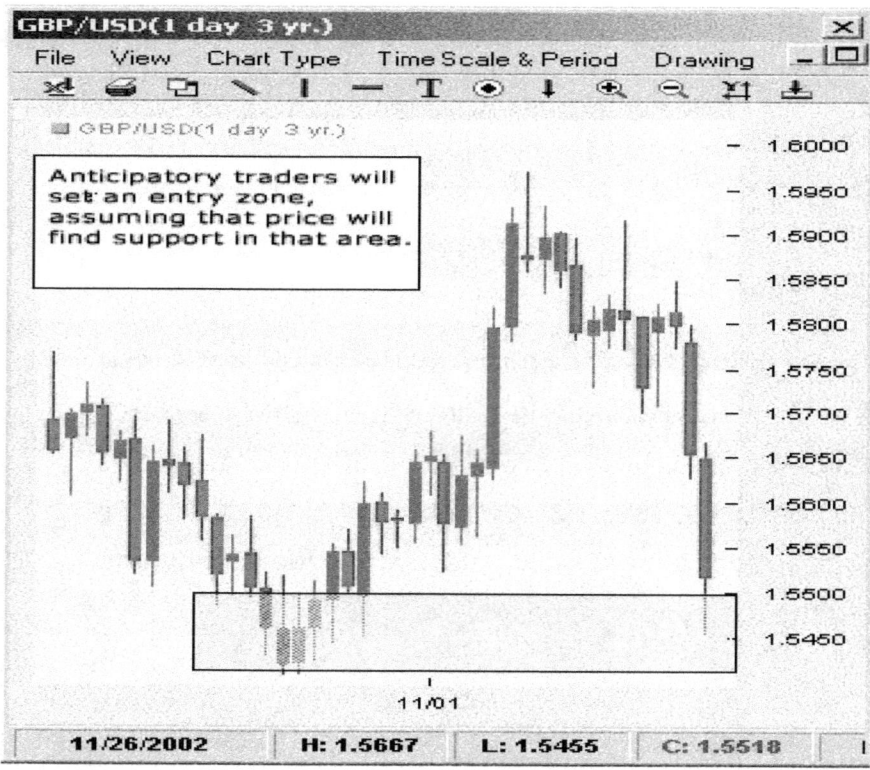

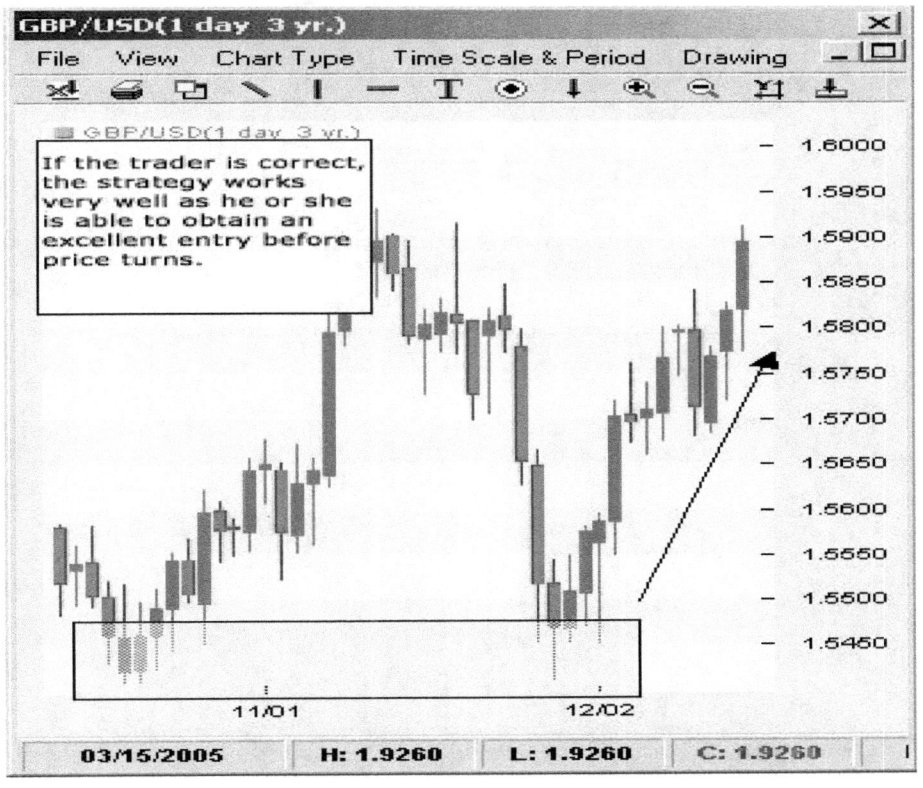

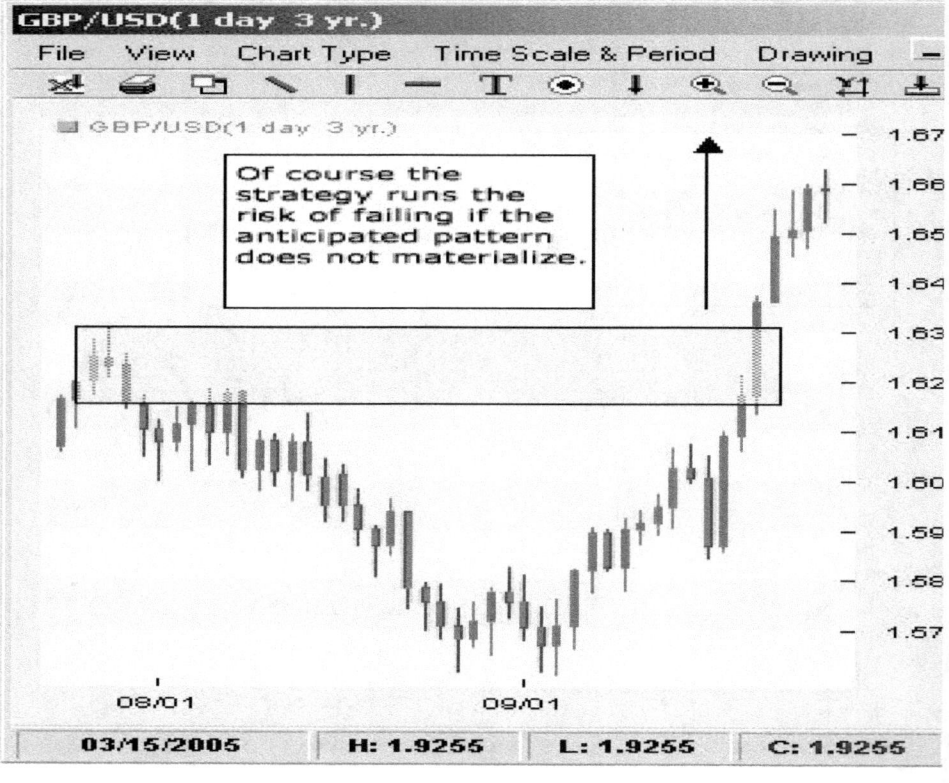

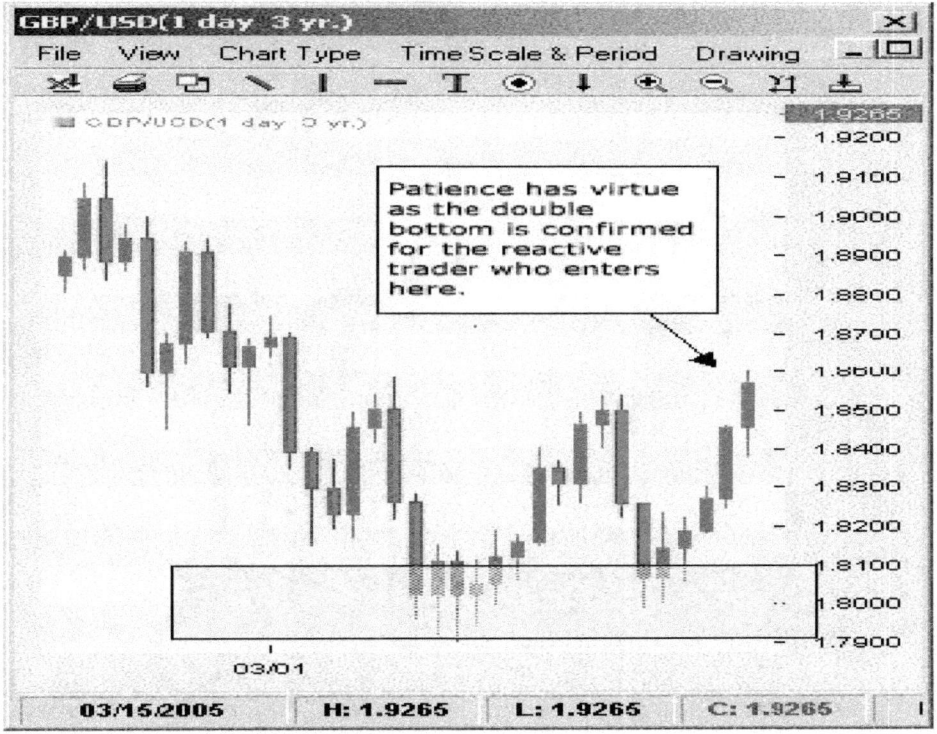

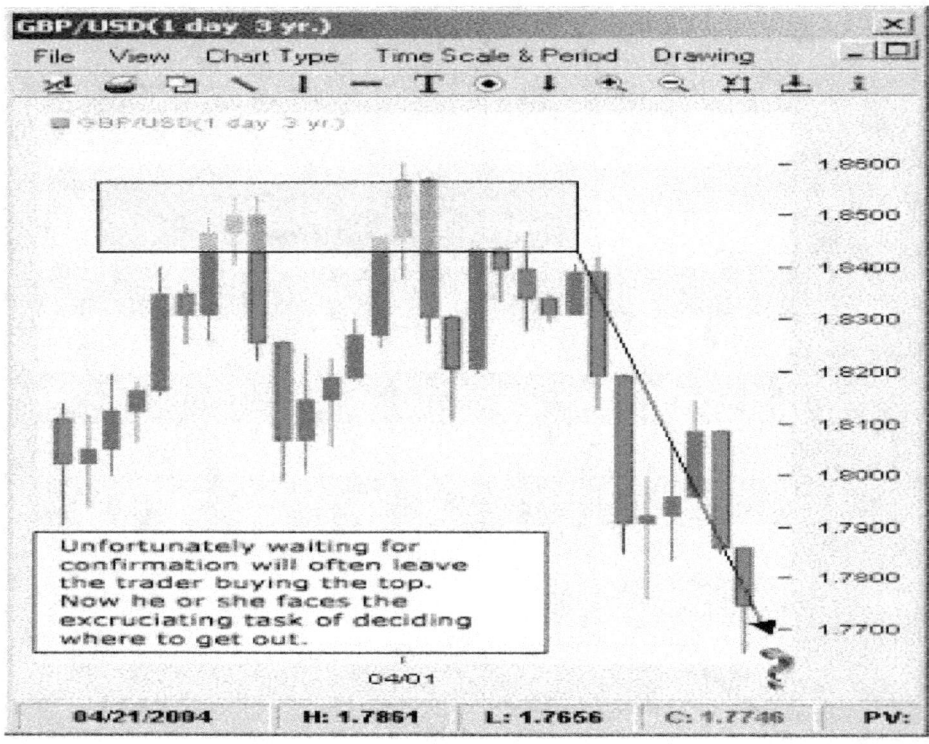

What's Obvious Is Not Often Right

Most traders are inclined to place a stop right at the bottom of a double bottom or top of the double top. The conventional wisdom says that once the pattern is broken, the trader should get out. But conventional wisdom is often wrong.

Leaving the trade early may seem prudent and logical, but markets are rarely that straightforward. Many retail traders play double tops/bottoms, and, knowing this, dealers and institutional traders love to exploit the retail traders' behavior of exiting early, forcing the weak hands out of the trade before price changes direction. The net effect is a series of frustrating stops out of positions that often would have turned out to be successful trades.

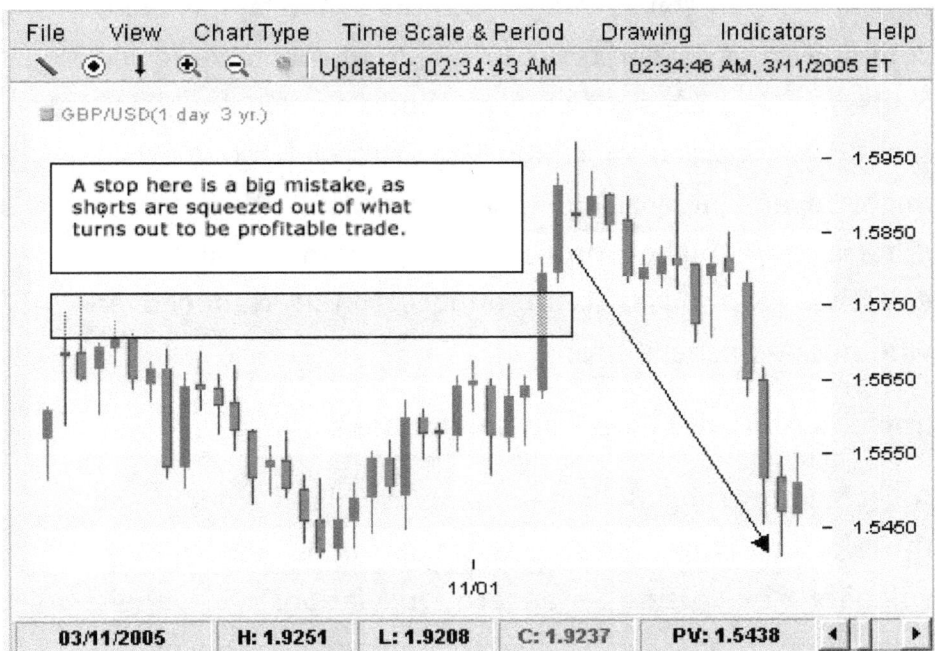

What Are Stops For?

Most traders make the mistake of using stops for risk control. But risk control in trading should be achieved through proper position size, not stops. The general rule of thumb is never to risk more than 2% of capital per trade. For smaller traders, that can sometimes mean ridiculously small trades.

Fortunately, in FX where many dealers allow flexible lot sizes, down to one unit per lot - the 2% rule of thumb is easily possible. Nevertheless, many traders insist on using tight stops on highly leveraged positions. In fact, it is quite common for a trader to generate 10 consecutive losing trades under such tight stop methods. So, we could say that in FX, instead of controlling risk, ineffective stops might even increase it. Their function, then, is to determine the highest probability for a point of failure. An effective stop poses little doubt to the trader over whether he or she is wrong.

Implementing the True Function of Stops

A technique using Bollinger Bands can help traders set those proper stops. Because Bollinger Bands® incorporate volatility by using standard deviations in their calculations, they can accurately project price levels at which traders should abandon their trades.

The method for using Bollinger-Bands stops for double tops and double bottoms are quite simple:

Isolate the point of the first top or bottom, and overlay Bollinger Bands with four-standard-deviation parameters.

Draw a line from the first top or bottom to the Bollinger Band. The point of intersection becomes your stop.

At first glance, four standard deviations may seem like an extreme choice. After all, two standard deviations cover

95% of possible scenarios in a normal distribution of a dataset. However, all those who have traded financial markets know that price action is anything but normal - if it were, the type of crashes that happen in financial markets every five or 10 years would occur only once every 6,000 years. Classic statistical assumptions are not very useful for traders. Therefore setting a wider standard deviation parameter is a must.

Using Bollinger Band® "Bands" To Gauge Trends

The four standard deviations cover more than 99% of all probabilities and therefore seem to offer a reasonable cut-off point. More importantly, they work well in actual testing, providing stops that are not too tight, yet not so wide as to become prohibitively costly. Note how well they work on the following GBP/USD example.

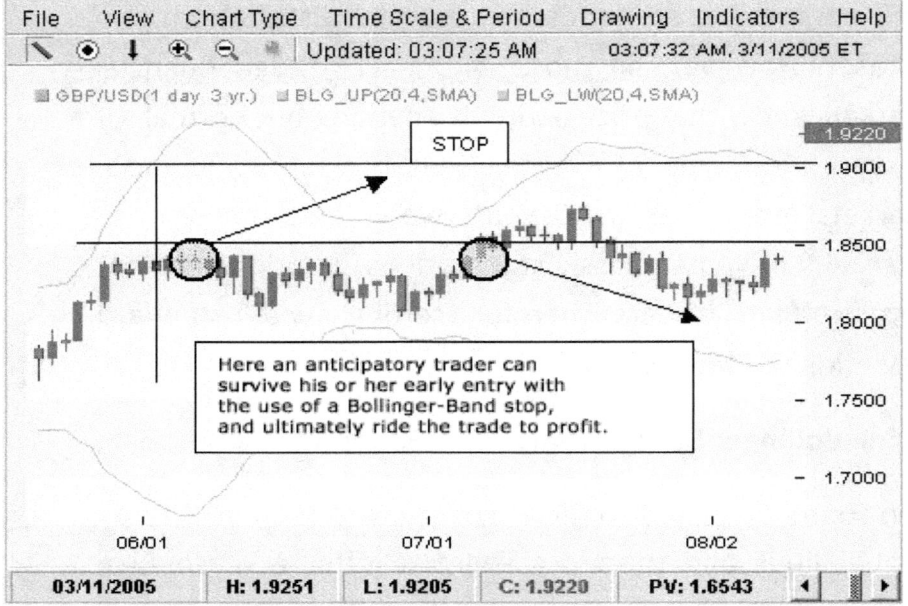

More importantly, take a look at the next example. A true sign of a proper stop is a capacity to protect the trader from runaway losses. In the following chart, the trade is clearly wrong but is stopped out well before the one-way move causes major damage to the trader's account.

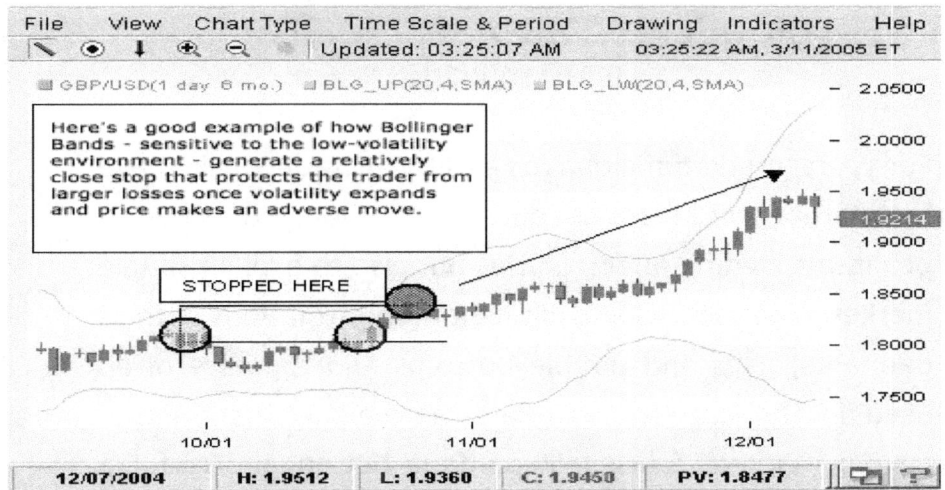

The Bottom Line

The genius of Bollinger Bands is their adaptability. By constantly incorporating volatility, they adjust quickly to the rhythm of the market. Using them to set proper stops when trading double bottoms and double tops - the most frequent price patterns in FX - makes those common trades much more effective.

INTRODUCING THE DIAMOND BEARISH FORMATION

For years, market aficionados and forex traders alike have been using simple price patterns not only to forecast profitable trading opportunities but also to explain simple market dynamics. As a result, common formations such as pennants, flags and double bottoms and tops are often used in the currency markets, as well as many other trading markets. A less talked about, but equally useful, a pattern that occurs in the currency markets is the bearish diamond top formation, commonly known as the diamond top. In this article, we'll explain how forex traders can quickly identify diamond tops in order to capitalize on various opportunities.

The diamond top occurs mostly at the top of considerable uptrends. It effectively signals impending shortfalls and retracements with relative accuracy and ease. Because of the increased liquidity of the currency market, this formation can be easier to identify in the currency market than in its equity-based counterpart, where gaps in price action frequently occur, displacing some of the requirements needed to recognize the diamond top. This formation can also be applied to any time frame, especially daily and hourly charts, as the wide swings often seen in the currency markets, will offer traders plenty of opportunities to trade.

Identifying and Trading the Formation

The diamond top formation is established by first isolating an off-center head-and-shoulders formation and applying trendlines dependent on the subsequent peaks and troughs. It gets its name from the fact that the pattern bears a striking resemblance to a four-sided diamond.

Let's look at a step-by-step breakdown of how to trade the formation, using the Australian dollar/U.S. dollar (AUD/USD) currency pair (Figure 1) as our example. First, we identify an off-center head-and-shoulders formation in a currency pair. Next, we draw resistance trendlines, first from the left shoulder to the head (line A) and then from the head to the right shoulder (line B). This forms the top of the formation; as a result, the price action should not break above the upper trendline resistance formed by the right shoulder. The idea is that the price action consolidates before the impending shortfall, and any penetrations above the trendline would ultimately make the pattern ineffective, as it would mean that a new peak has been created. As a result, the trader would be forced to consider either reapplying the trend line (line B) that runs from the head to the right shoulder, or disregarding the diamond top formation altogether, since the pattern has been broken.

To establish lower trendline support, the technician will simply eye the lowest trough established in the formation. Bottom side support can then be drawn by connecting the bottom tail to the left shoulder (line C) and then connecting another support trendline from the tail to the right shoulder (line D). This connects the bottom half to the top and completes the pattern. Notice how the rightmost angle of the formation also resembles the apex of a symmetrical triangle pattern and is suggestive of a breakout.

Figure 1 - Identifying a diamond top formation using the AUD/USD.

Trading the diamond top isn't much harder than trading other formations. Here, the trader is simply looking for a break of the lower support line, suggesting increasing momentum for a probable shortfall. The theory is quite simple. Both upper resistance and lower support levels established by the right shoulder will contain the price action as each subsequent session's range diminishes, suggestive of a near-term breakout. Once a session closes below the support level, this indicates that selling momentum will continue because sellers have finally pushed the close below this significant mark. The trader will then want to place his/her entry shortly below this level to capture the subsequent decline in the price. This approach works especially well in the currency markets, where price action tends to be more fluid and trends are established more quickly once a certain significant support or resistance level is broken. Money management would be applied to this position through a stop-loss placed slightly above the previously broken support level to minimize any losses that might occur if the break is false and a temporary retracement takes place.

Figure 2 below shows a zoomed-in view of Figure 1. We can see that a session candle closed below or "broke" the support trend line (line D.i.), indicating a move lower. The diamond top trader would profit from this by placing an entry order below the close of the support line at 0.7504, while also placing a stop-loss slightly above the same line to minimize any potential losses should the price bounce back above. The standard stop will be placed 50 pips higher at 0.7554. In our example, the stop order would not have been executed because the price did not bounce back, instead of falling 150 pips lower in one session before falling even further later on.

Source: FX Trek Intellicharts   Copyright © 2005 Investopedia.com

Figure 2 - A closer look at the diamond top formation using the AUD/USD. Notice how the position of the entry is just below the support line (D.i.).

Finally, profit targets are calculated by taking the width of the formation from the head of the formation (the highest price) to the bottom of the tail (the lowest price). Staying with our example using the AUD/USD currency pair, Figure 3 shows how this would be done. In Figure 3, the AUD/USD exchange rate at the top of the formation is

0.8003. The bottom of the diamond top is exactly 0.7250. This leaves 753 pips between the two prices that we use to form the maximum price where we can take profits. To be safe, the trader will set two targets in which to take profits. The first target will require taking the full amount, 753 pips, and taking half that amount and subtracting it from our entry price. Then, the first target will be 0.7128. The price target that will maximize our profits will be 0.6751, calculated by subtracting the full 753 pips from the entry price.

Figure 3 - The price target is calculated on the same example of the AUD/USD.

Using a Price Oscillator Helps

One of the cardinal rules of successful trading is to always receive confirmation, and the diamond top pattern is no different. Adding a price oscillator such as moving average convergence divergence and the relative strength index can increase the accuracy of your trade since tools like these can gauge price action momentum and be used to confirm the break of support or resistance.

Getting To Know Oscillators

Applying the stochastic oscillator to our example (Figure 4 below), the investor confirms the break below support through the downward cross that occurs in the price oscillator (point X).

Figure 4 - The cross of the stochastic momentum indicator (point X) is used to confirm the downward move.

Putting It All Together

Not only do bearish diamond tops form in the major currency pairs like the Euro/U.S. dollar (EUR/USD), the British pound/U.S. dollar (GBP/USD) and the U.S. dollar/Japanese yen (USD/JPY), but they also form in lesser-known cross-currency pairs such as the Euro/Japanese yen (EUR/JPY). Although the formation occurs less in the cross-currency pairs, the swings tend to last longer, creating more profits. Let's look at a step-by-step example of this using the EUR/JPY:

Identify the head and shoulders pattern and confirm the offset nature of the formation by noticing that the head is slight to the left, while the tail is set to the right.

From the top resistance by connecting the left shoulder to the tip top of the head (line A) and the head to the right shoulder (line B). Next, draw the trendlines for support by connecting the left shoulder (line C) to the tail and the tail to the right shoulder (line D).

Calculate the width of the formation by taking the prices at the top of the head, 141.59, and the bottom of the tail, 132.94. This will give us a total of 865 pips of distance before we can take our full profits. Divide by two and our first point to take profits will be 432 pips below our entry.

Establish the entry point. Look to the apex of the right shoulder and notice the point where the candle closes below the support line, breaking through. Here, the close of the session is 137.79. The entry order should then be placed 50 pips below at 137.29, while our stop-loss order will be placed 50 pips above at 137.79.

Calculate the first take profit price by subtracting 432 pips from the entry. As a result, the first profit target will be at 133.45.

Finally, confirm the trade by using a price oscillator. Here, the stochastic oscillator signals ahead and confirm the opportunity as it breaks below overbought levels (point X).

If the first target is achieved, the trader will move his/her stop up to the first target, then place a trailing stop to protect any further profits.

Source: FX Trek Intellicharts   Copyright © 2005 Investopedia.com

Figure 5 - A different example of a diamond top formation using the EUR/JPY cross-currency pair. This chart shows all the trendlines, the highest and the lowest price, and the price target.

The Bottom Line

Although the bearish diamond top has been overlooked due to its infrequency, it remains very effective in displaying potential opportunities in the forex market. Smoother price action due to the enormous liquidity of the market offers traders a better context in which to apply this method and isolate better opportunities. When this formation is combined with a price oscillator, the trade becomes an even better catch - the price oscillator enhances the overall likelihood of a profitable trade by gauging price momentum and confirming weakness as well as weeding out false breakout/breakdown trades.

MOMENTUM

One of the key tenets of technical analysis is that price frequently lies, but momentum generally speaks the truth. Just as professional poker players play the player and not the cards, professional traders trade momentum rather than price. In forex (FX), a robust momentum model can be an invaluable tool for trading, but traders often grapple with the question of what type of model to use. Here we look at how you can design a simple and effective momentum model in FX using the moving average convergence divergence (MACD) histogram.

Why Momentum?

First, we need to look at why momentum is so important to trading. A good way to understand the significance of momentum is to step outside of the financial markets altogether and look at an asset class that has experienced rising prices for a very long time - housing. House prices are measured in two ways: month-over-month increases and year-over-year increases. If house prices in New York were higher in November than in October, then we could safely conclude that demand for housing remained firm and further increases were likely. However, if prices in November suddenly declined from prices paid in October, especially after relentlessly rising for most of the year, then that might provide the first clue to a possible change of trend. Sure, house prices would most likely still be higher in a year-over-year comparison, lulling the general public into believing that the real estate market was still buoyant. However, real estate professionals, who are well aware that weakness in housing manifests itself far earlier in month-over-month figures than in year-over-year data, would be far more reluctant to buy under those conditions.

In real estate, month-over-month figures provide a measure of the rate of change, which is what the study of momentum is all about. Much like their counterparts in the real estate market, professionals in the financial markets will keep a closer eye on momentum than they do on price to ascertain the true direction of a move.

Using the MACD Histogram To Measure Momentum

The rate of change can be measured in a variety of ways in technical analysis; a relative strength index (RSI), a commodity channel index (CCI) or a stochastic oscillator can all be used to gauge momentum. However, for the purposes of this story, the MACD histogram is the technical indicator of choice. (To learn more, see Moving Average Convergence Divergence - Part 2.)

First invented by Gerry Appel in the 1970s, the MACD is one of the simplest, yet most effective, technical indicators around. When used in FX, it simply records the difference between the 26-period exponential moving average (EMA) and the 12-period exponential moving average of a currency pair. (To learn more, see Trading The MACD Divergence and Basics Of Weighted Moving Averages.) In addition, a nine-period EMA of MACD itself is plotted alongside the MACD and acts as a trigger line. When MACD crosses the nine-period line from the bottom, it signifies a change to the upside; when the move happens in the opposite manner, a downside signal is made.

This oscillation of the MACD around the nine-period line was first plotted into a histogram format by Thomas Aspray in 1986 and became known as the MACD histogram. Although the histogram is, in fact, a derivative of a derivative, it can be deadly accurate as a potential guide to price direction. Here is one way to design a simple momentum model in FX using the MACD histogram.

1. The first and most important step are to define a MACD segment. For a long position, a MACD segment is simply the full cycle made by the MACD histogram from the initial breach of the 0 line from the underside to the final collapse through the 0 line from the topside. For a short, the rules are simply reversed. Figure 1 shows an example of a MACD segment in the EUR/USD currency pair.

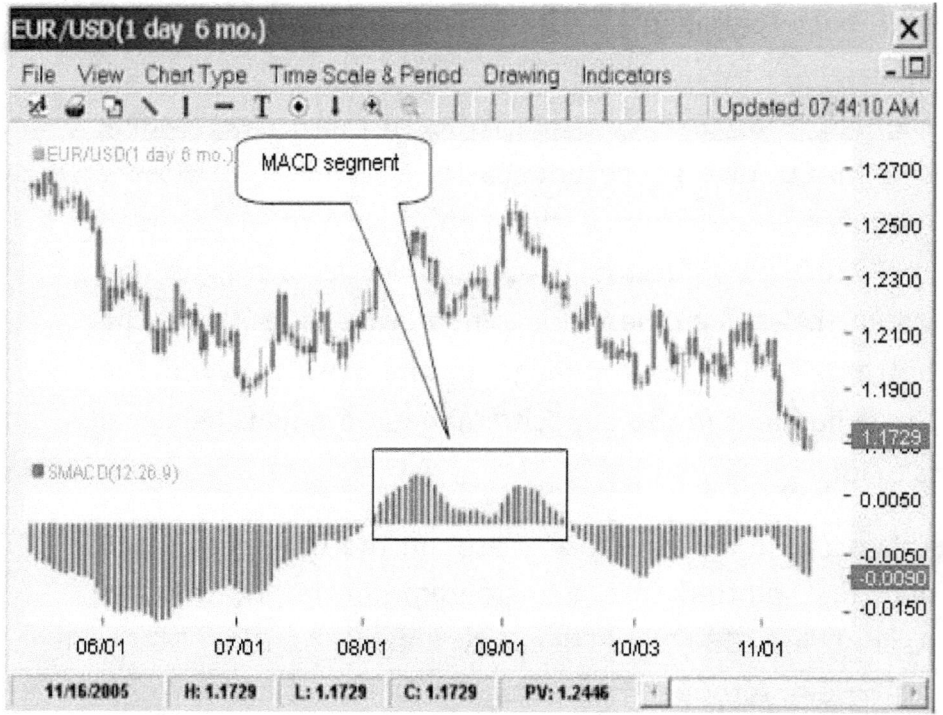

2. Once the MACD segment is established, you need to measure the value of the highest bar within that segment to record the momentum reference point. In the case of a short, the process is simply reversed.

3. Having noted the prior high (or low) in the preceding segment, you can then use that value to construct the model. Moving on to Figure 2, we can see that the preceding MACD high was .0027. If the MACD histogram now registers a downward reading whose absolute value exceeds .0027, then we will know that downward momentum has exceeded upward momentum, and we'll

conclude that the present set-up presents a high probability short.

If the case were reversed and the preceding MACD segment were negative, a positive reading in the present segment that would exceed the lowest low of the prior segment would then signal a high probability long.

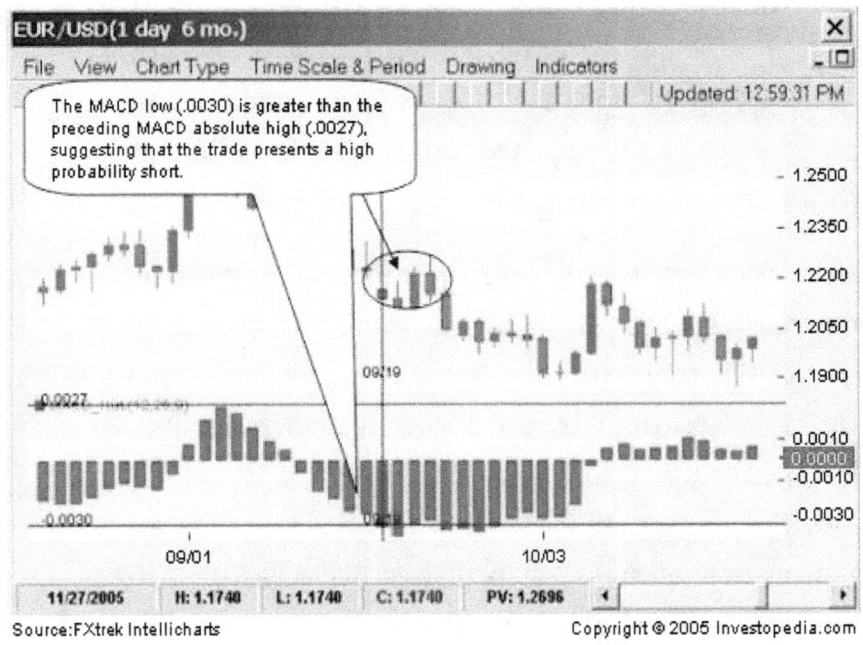

Figure 2

What is the logic behind this idea? The basic premise is that momentum, as signified by the MACD histogram, can provide clues to the underlying direction of the market. Using the assumption that momentum precedes price, the thesis of the set-up is simply this: a new swing high in momentum should lead to a new swing high in price, and vice versa. Let's think about why this makes sense. A new momentum swing low or high is usually created when price makes a sudden and violent move in one direction. What precipitates such price action? A belief by either bulls or bears that price at present levels represents inordinate value, and therefore strong profit opportunity. Typically, these are the early buyers or sellers, and they wouldn't be acting so quickly if they didn't believe that price was going to make a substantive move in that direction. Generally, it pays to follow their lead, because this group often represents the "smart money crowd".

However, although this set-up may indeed offer a high probability of success, it is by no means a guaranteed money-making opportunity. Not only will the set-up sometimes fail outright by producing false signals, but it can also generate a losing trade even if the signal is accurate. Remember that while momentum indicates a strong presence of trend, it provides no measure of its ultimate potential. In other words, we may be relatively certain of the direction of the move, but not of its amplitude. As with most trading set-ups, the successful use of the momentum model is much more a matter of art than science.

Looking at Entry Strategies

A trader can employ several different entry strategies with the momentum model. The simplest is to take a market long or market shortly when the model flashes a buy or a sell signal. This may work, but it often forces the trader to enter at the most inopportune time, as the signal is typically produced at the absolute top or bottom of the price burst. Prices may continue further in the direction of the trade, but it's far more likely that they will retrace and that the trader will have a better entry opportunity if he or she simply waits. Figure 3 demonstrates one such entry strategy.

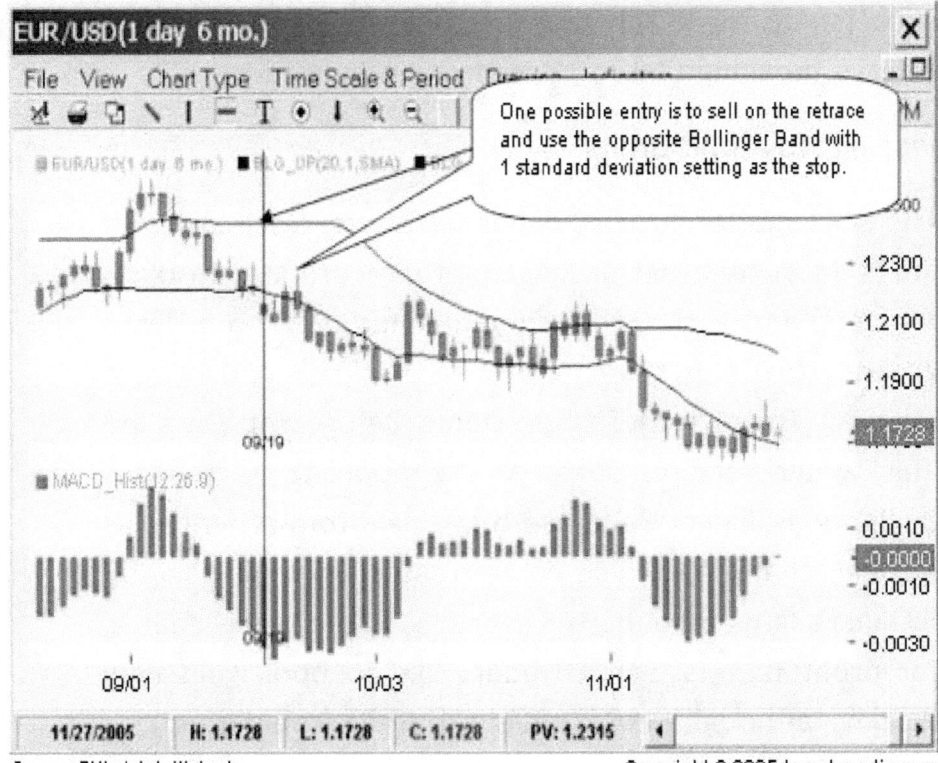

Figure 3

Sometimes price will retrace against the direction signal to a far greater degree than expected and yet the momentum signal will remain valid. In that case, some skilled traders will add to their positions - a practice that some traders have jokingly termed "SHADDing" (for "short add") or "LADDing" (for "long add"). For the novice trader, this can be a very dangerous maneuver - there is a possibility that you could end up adding to a bad trade and, therefore, compounding your losses, which could be disastrous. Experienced traders, however, know how to successfully "fight the tape" if they perceive that price offers a meaningful divergence from momentum.

Placing Stops and Limits

The final matter to consider is where to place stops or limits in such a set-up. Again, there are no absolute answers, and each trader should experiment on a demo account to determine his or her own risk and reward criteria. (To learn more, see Demo Before You Dive In.) This writer sets his stops at the opposite 1 standard deviation Bollinger Band® setting away from his entry, as he feels that if the price has retreated from his position by such a large amount, the set-up is quite likely to fail. As for profit targets, some traders like to book gain very quickly, although more patient traders could reap far larger rewards if the trade develops a strong directional move.

Conclusion

Traders often say that the best trade may be the one you don't take. One of the greatest strengths of the momentum model is that it does not engage in low probability set-ups. Traders can fall prey to the impulse to try to catch every single turn or move of the currency pair. The momentum model effectively inhibits such destructive behavior by keeping the trader away from the market when the countervailing momentum is too strong.

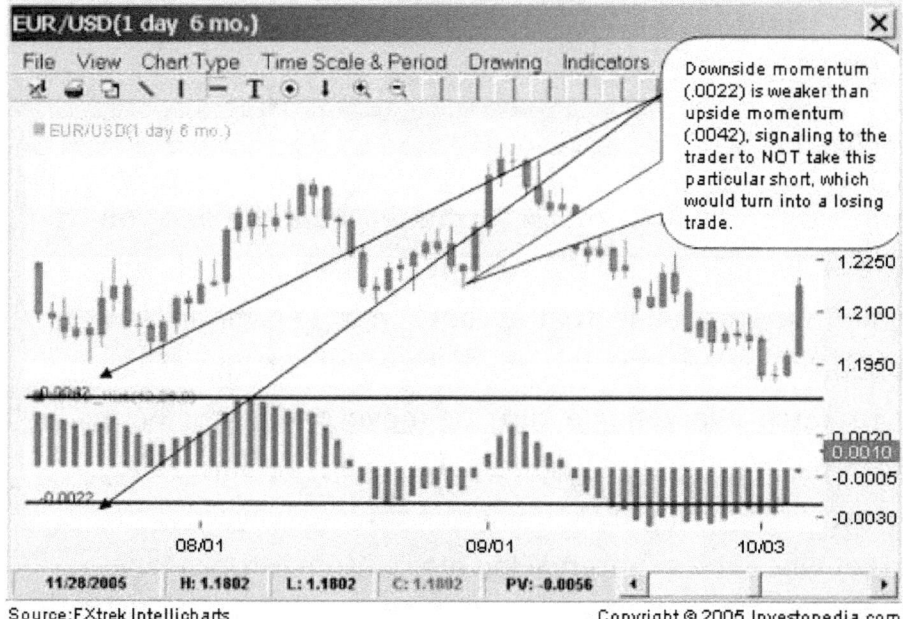

Figure 4

As Kenny Rogers once sang in "The Gambler", "You've got to know when to hold them, and you got to know when to fold them". In trading, as in poker, this is the true skill of the game. The simple momentum model we've described here is one tool that we hope will help currency traders improve their trade selection process and make smarter choices.

FOREX CONSOLIDATION

Much like the first dynamite compound invented by Swedish chemist and engineer Alfred Nobel, consolidation periods and patterns in the currency markets can explode, leading to great profit opportunities for the FX trader. Sometimes suggestive of indecision, consolidation periods are great for capturing potential because the burst of directional action that follows can last for an extended period.

Understanding and trading on consolidation patterns will give the currency trader in the know two "edges". First, the trader can hold his or her initial position for a shorter amount of time, thus minimizing the risk of holding positions in the case of higher rollover interest. Second, the profit potential from such a position can be big, as long as the trader follows strict, disciplined money management rules. Without money management, the trader might as well be playing with fire. Here we look at two different consolidation patterns and give you a step-by-step explanation of how to trade them.

The Flag - Continuation of the Trend

The flag formation is one of two consolidation patterns that can lead to great profit opportunities. Common in the currency markets, the flag formation serves as an indication of continuation (i.e. a continuation pattern).

This type of consolidation occurs after a significant uptrend and is usually referenced as a stopping point before further strengthening momentum ensues. With this type of formation, the duration of the consolidation period is rather short and tends to go against the previous uptrend direction.

Figure 1 presents an example of a flag formation in the GBP/JPY currency cross pair.

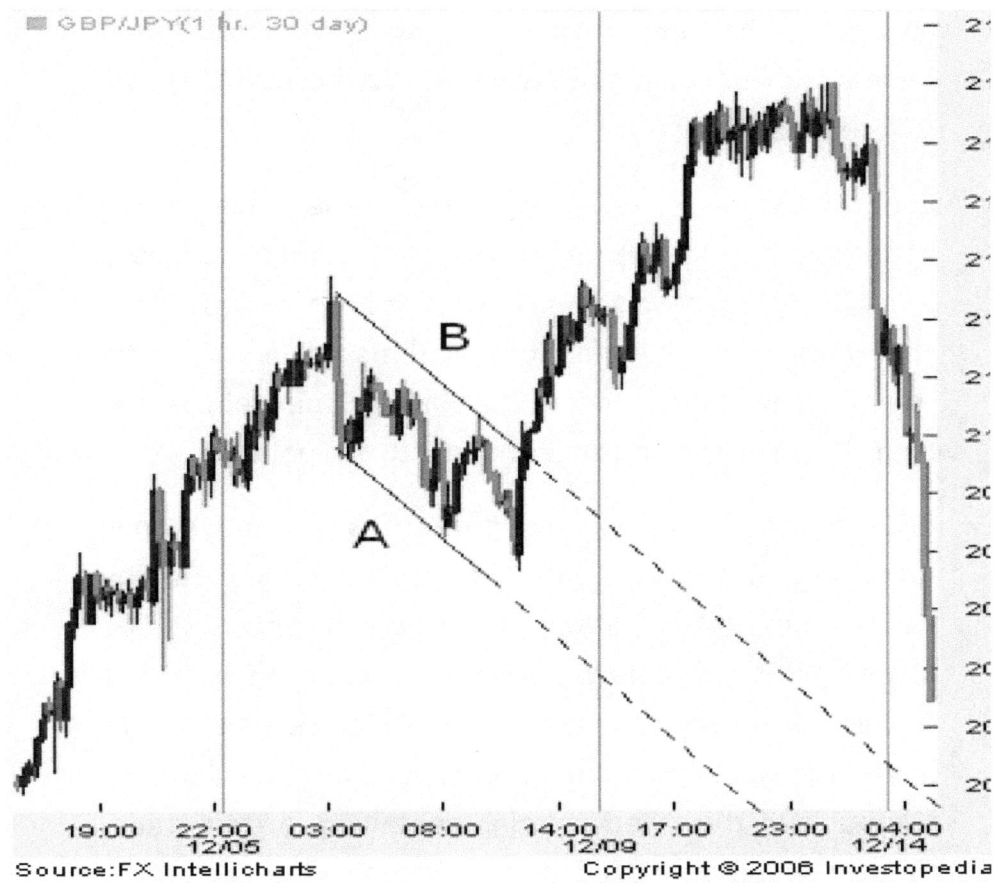

Figure 1 - A great continuation suggestion following the flag formation

Let's take a step-by-step approach to identifying and trading the flag formation seen in this chart:

Apply trendlines to accurately identify the flag formation: First, we establish the lower support trendline by connecting the lower wicks of the candles at point A. Then we establish the upper trendline at point B by connecting the topside wicks. Note that both lines should be relatively parallel - any deviation may be indicative of a different pattern.

Zoom into the exact points where the price action approaches either the upper or lower trendline: In Figure 2, we zoom in on an approach of the upper resistance ceiling. Once we have a close of the session above the trendline, the entry should be placed 5 pips above the high. This would place the entry at 210.10 (point X).

Always place a corresponding stop loss: Sound money management should always be applied to any trading position. In this situation, the stop-loss order will be placed two-thirds below the previous session's high. The underlying theory is simply that if the price breaks back below the upper trendline, the close above was simply a fakeout and the trend is being contained. In this trade, the stop would be placed at 209.77 (see Figure 2).

Taking a short-term stance: Here, a trader can hold for the day and close the trade before the New York markets close in order to avoid the rollover on the position. If the trader takes advantage of the short-term explosion, he or she has the potential to capture 95 pips (profiting from the high at 211.05) while maintaining a 2:1 risk-reward ratio. But the trader can also opt to hold on to longer-term gains. If the trader holds on longer, he or she could realize a much larger profit - in this example, the move topped out at 213.

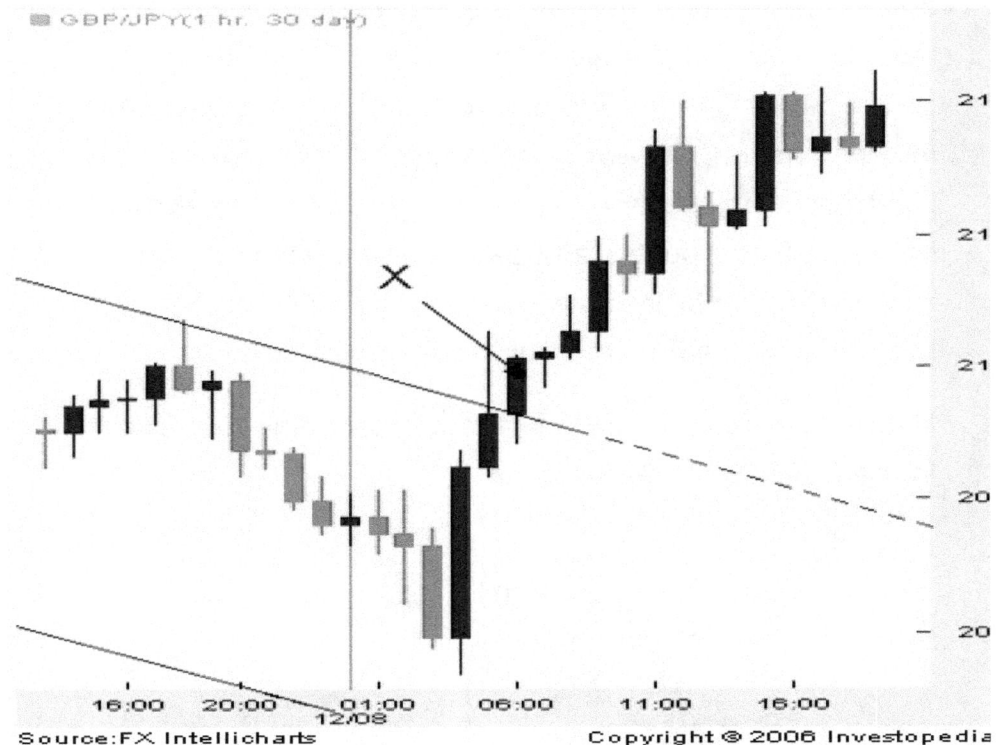

Figure 2 - X marks the perfect entry.

The Broadening Formation - Consolidation before the Reverse

Like the flag formation, the broadening formation - our second consolidation pattern of choice - is also found in an uptrend, but it indicates a reversal of the trend, rather than a continuation. Similar to a staid rectangular consolidation pattern, the broadening formation is great for establishing a top in an uptrend or a bottom in a downtrend, and it is thus suggestive of a near-term reversal in the price action. Here, traders are consolidating their positions by establishing an upper and lower trendline. However, the swings become longer and larger as compared to earlier fluctuations. The strong battle between buyers and sellers ultimately ends when the price action breaks the lower (or upper) boundary and bearish (or bullish) momentum are established.

Figure 3 presents an example of a broadening formation in the AUD/USD major pair.

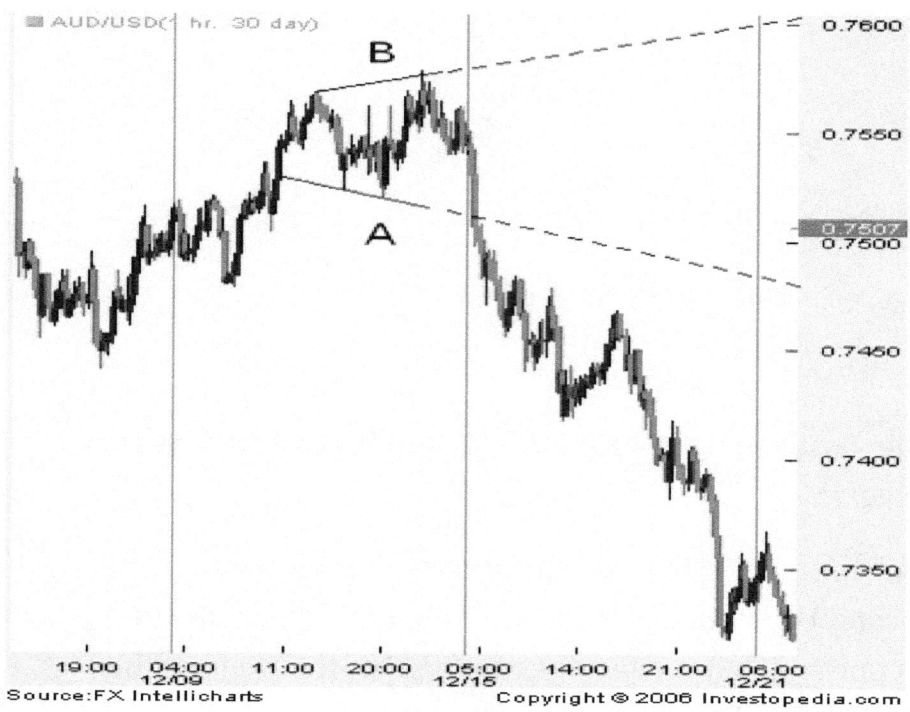

Figure 3 - Textbook broadening formation leads to explosive gains.

Let's take a step-by-step approach to a shorter time frame application of the broadening formation in this chart:

Identify the broadening formation through diverging trend lines: Before trading the formation, it's important to clearly establish the pattern. Here in Figure 3, we apply the lower trendline by connecting the lower wicks at point A. Then we connect the topside wicks at point B. Rather than run parallel as they do in the flag formation, the trendlines in this formation will diverge. It's important to see that divergence - otherwise, another formation or pattern may be in the works, misleading the trader.

Apply the entry at the exact break: In Figure 4, we zoom in and see the close below the bottom trendline. This is suggestive of a break, so a currency trader would place the entry 5 pips below the low of the session. In this example, this would put the entry at 0.7493 (point X).

Use proper money management: We can't forget to apply disciplined money management here, so a stop loss will be added 30 pips above where the lower trendline crosses through the closed session. In this case, the trendline would be placed at 0.7511 and our subsequent stop at 0.7541. With 48 pips of the room, due to the stop-loss order, we are now looking for a minimum of 96 pips in maintaining a 2:1 risk-reward ratio.

Taking a longer-term stance: Although offering a short-term direction in price, the broadening formation tends to spark longer-term trends. As a result, in this case, a trader may decide to take profits at 0.7445 (a 1:1 risk-reward) or hold on to the longer-term position. In the case of the longer term, the spot price declines before establishing a bottom at 0.7266 - nearly 230 pips from the entry, and a more than adequate 2:1 risk-reward ratio.

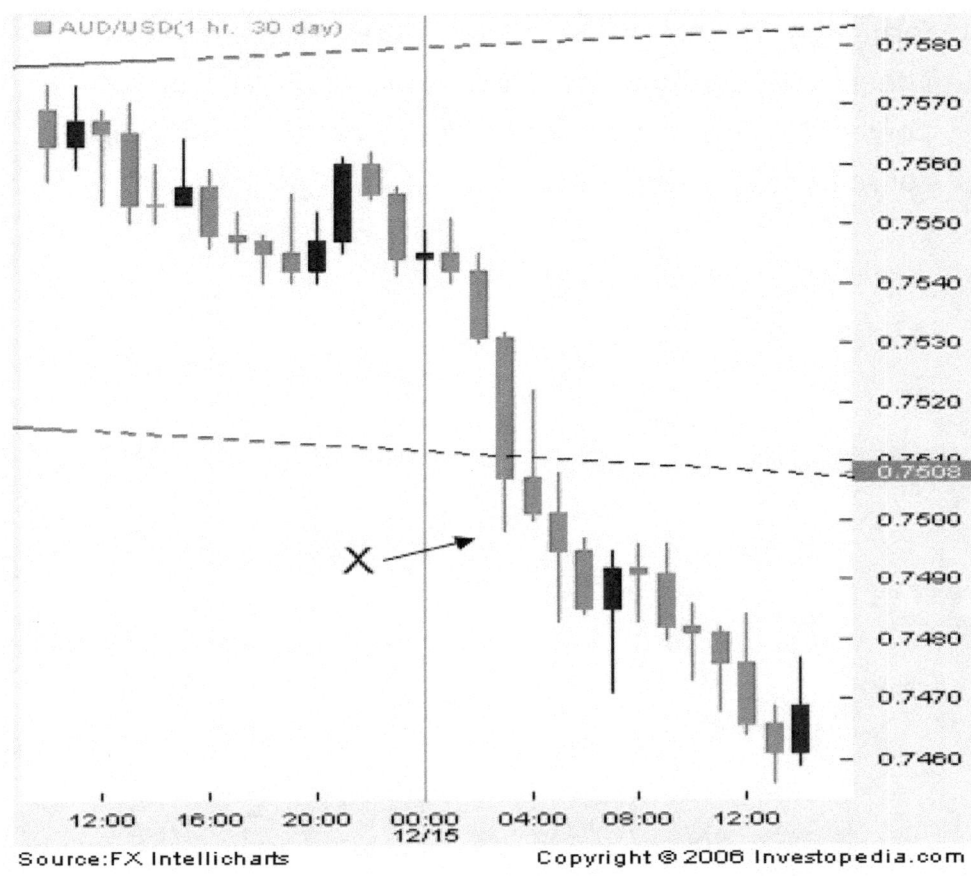

Figure 4 - X marks a great entry for profit potential.

Conclusion

Both of these consolidation patterns and their corresponding strategies can be executed by both the novice and the expert trader, allowing the individual to isolate great potential profit opportunities in a short amount of time. The flag formation offers opportunities to trade on a continuation basis, while the broadening formation offers opportunities in reversal situations. Either way, the trader will be taking advantage of the powerful directional bias that occurs following consolidative neutrality

SUMMARY

While this forex ebook only represents a fraction of all there is to know about forex trading, we hope that you've gained some insight into this topic. We also encourage those of you who are interested in potentially trading in the forex market to learn more about the complexities and intricacies that make this market unique.

Let's recap:

The forex market represents the electronic over-the-counter markets where currencies are traded worldwide 24 hours a day, five and a half days a week. The typical means of trading forex are on the spot, futures and forwards markets.

Currencies are "priced" in currency pairs and are quoted either directly or indirectly.

Currencies typically have two prices: bid (the amount that the market will buy the quote currency for in relation to the base currency); and ask (the amount the market will sell one unit of the base currency for in relation to the quote currency). The bid price is always smaller than the asking price.

Unlike conventional equity and debt markets, forex investors have access to large amounts of leverage, which allows substantial positions to be taken without making a large initial investment.

The adoption and elimination of several global currency systems over time led to the formation of the present currency exchange system, in which most countries use some measure of floating exchange rates.

Governments, central banks, banks and other financial institutions, hedgers, and speculators are the main players in the forex market.

The main economic theories found in the foreign exchange deal with parity conditions such as those involving interest rates and inflation. Overall, a country's qualitative and quantitative factors are seen as large influences on its currency in the forex market.

Forex traders use fundamental analysis to view currencies and their countries like companies, thereby using economic announcements to gain an idea of the currency's true value.

Forex traders use technical analysis to look at currencies the same way they would any other asset and, therefore, use technical tools such as trends, charts, and indicators in their trading strategies.

Unlike stock trades, forex trades have minimal commissions and related fees. But new forex traders should take a conservative approach and use orders, such as the take-profit or stop-loss, to minimize losses.

www.ingramcontent.com/pod-product-compliance
Lightning Source LLC
Chambersburg PA
CBHW070104210526
45170CB00012B/738